Well, I suppose I'm not that good

Yes, I know I am not perfect.

Alright, I have to admit that I can't make myself the person I should be.

I suppose I have to confess that at times I have also deliberately acted in a bad way, thought unworthy thoughts, said wrong things, wanted what was wrong, and that my motives also have been questionable.

In fact, I have to admit I am a failure

Alright, let's face the truth: I have broken God's Ten Commandments.

1 I am selfish at heart.
I matter more to me than anyone else.

2 I do not even try to put God first in my life.

3 My language is sometimes bad.
I have used the name of 'God' and 'Jesus' wrongly sometimes.

4 I have not bothered to keep Sunday in the way God wants me to. It has been a day for me, not for Him.

Furthermore

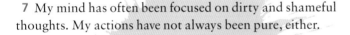

5 I have not always treated my parents properly.

6 I have hated others in my heart: sometimes this has made me act wrongly towards them.

7 My mind has often been focused on dirty and shameful thoughts. My actions have not always been pure, either.

8 I have stolen from others.

9 I find it easy to lie—especially when something is at stake.

10 I am guilty of envy and jealousy. I find myself wanting to have what others have got.

Sometimes

Sometimes my failures have not worried me at all.

Unless, of course, I have been found out, and there have been bad consequences for me.

Sometimes I have had twinges of conscience, and wondered

'Why am I like this?'

Other times, I have felt really bad and dirty inside.

I have asked myself 'Why does my heart seem so rotten?'

My question

Occasionally my question within has been:

'What does God think of me?'

That three-letter word

The Bible says what God is like.

It tells me what He thinks of me.

It says He is pure, righteous, and holy.

It tells us that He hates all those wrong things of which I am guilty.

It calls them by a simple word of three letters: 'sin'.

It is like a blot on my life.

The perfect Judge

It says that God is an everlasting, perfect and righteous judge.

In any country, even the wisest and cleverest judges can make mistakes. They may misunderstand the facts. They may wrongly apply the law. They can get it wrong sometimes.

God never gets it wrong.

He sees the sins in our hearts as well as in our actions.

He sees them all: we cannot hide anything from Him.

No appeal

A judge must impose a penalty on someone who is guilty.

The penalty is not always correct: there are sometimes successful appeals against a wrong penalty.

But God never makes a mistake when He judges sin. He knows all the facts. He sees all our intentions. His standard is perfection. He hates sin and will pass His penalty on it.

There is no appeal from His penalty, because He is never wrong.

Unspoiled

In any legal system, there are many different penalties—and they change from time to time.

God has one penalty only. It never changes.

Because God is pure and hates sin, and because He is eternal and lives forever, His penalty means that no unforgiven sinner can ever spend eternity with Him in Heaven.

He will not allow the purity of Heaven to be spoiled in the way that this world has been spoiled by sin.

The exclusion clause

In Heaven there will be joy, peace, light, love, truth, real heartfelt worship, and the privilege of being with the Lord Jesus—and all those He has saved—forever and ever.

There will be no crying, no tears, no pain and no regrets there!

In fact, there will be no selfishness, no neglecting God, no ignoring His day, no disrespect to parents, no hatred in heart or action, no immorality in thought or deed, no stealing, no lying, and no envy and jealousy.

Wait a minute! The Bible says that none of the things that I find in myself will be found in Heaven.

That means that I will not be in Heaven—unless I am forgiven. The Bible says that no-one who tells even **one** lie—or whose life is really a lie—can enter Heaven.

The stark contrast

We don't like to admit it, but the Bible teaches that the only alternative to Heaven is a place called Hell. Sometimes we use the word unthinkingly, but it is important to know what it means, so we do not go there.

Hell is for unforgiven sinners.
Heaven and Hell have two things in common: first, they both last forever; second, no-one there will ever leave or be able to leave.

But there are two big differences between Heaven and Hell: first, Heaven will be loved while Hell will be hated by those present there; second, Heaven is a place of everlasting blessing while Hell is a place of everlasting punishment.

14

The BIG question

The important question now is:

How can God accept me?

How can God, who **is** love, love me when I have offended Him by my sin?

How can I avoid His punishment in Hell?

How can I enjoy His Heaven with Him?

How can I be 'saved'?

How can I know I am forgiven?

How can God accept **me?**

Now, will you let ME give YOU some answers, please?

No entry!

Let me first tell you how you **cannot** become accepted by God.

God cannot accept you just because you are **sincere**. Many sincere people are wrong about all kinds of things.

God cannot accept you simply because you are **religious** or **meet religious people in a religious building.**
We all know that there are as many hypocrites in churches and religious buildings as outside them.

God cannot accept you only because you have been **baptized** or **confirmed** or because you have been **through a ceremony** of another religion.
Outward things do not change our sinful hearts.

God cannot accept you because you have **done good things**.
You still need to have your sins forgiven.

All these ways spell 'No entry!'

In that case, **how can** God accept me?

Can a judge step into the dock?

Remember we said that a judge must impose a penalty when someone is found guilty?

Remember we saw that God, as Judge, finds us guilty—in our hearts and in our actions?

It would be unheard of, and impossible, for a judge to leave the bench and come down into the dock instead of the guilty man, or woman, and accept the verdict and the penalty in his, or her, place.

But that is how I became accepted by God in Jesus Christ.

Let me explain how it worked out for me.

The songs say it clearly

One song talks about Jesus, the eternal
Son of God who became man, and it says:

'He knew how sinful I had been.
He knew that God must punish sin.
So out of pity, Jesus said
He'd take the punishment instead'

Another one teaches about Jesus, who never sinned Himself
and thus had no sins of His own to pay for, and it states:

'There was no other good enough
To pay the price of sin.
He, only, could unlock the gates
Of Heaven and let me in'

'Most important of all'

It is amazing that God took on a human body and became a man. That is who Jesus of Nazareth was: God in the flesh, or 'Emmanuel'.

He lived a perfect life. Unlike my life, His was totally acceptable and pleasing to God The Father.

He loved people. He healed the sick, gave sight to the blind, opened the ears of the deaf, and raised the dead. He taught God's holy and right standards. He had power to work miracles, when it was right to do so.

But, most important of all, He went to the cross. That was a place of execution. He allowed Himself to be unjustly executed there by sinful men, for wrongs He had never done.

But He died there for guilty sinners like you and me.

'In my place'

I look back to that cross and see that all my sins were laid on Jesus, and that God the Father punished Him in my place.

The Lord Jesus Christ willingly accepted, in His body on the cross, the eternal wrath and judgement that I deserve, so that I could go free.

Three days later God the Father raised His Son from the dead.

He walked the earth showing unmistakable proofs of His resurrection, then ascended into Heaven at the right hand of the Father.

One day He will come again, in power and great glory.

But I rush ahead! Let's get back to how God dealt with **me**—and how He can deal with **you**.

The way up, is down!

I began to understand what Jesus had done for me on the cross.

I could be completely cleansed and forgiven when I admitted my sin and my wrongdoing and turned to Him personally to save me and to become my Lord and Friend.

Also the truth dawned that I was morally bankrupt before God, because of my many failures. But Jesus was perfect in every way.

When I turned to Him He filled my empty life with all the richness of what He is worth. His measureless value was put to my credit in my bankrupt account.

I was accepted because of Him

This was solely because of who Jesus is and what He had done for me, and not because of anything I had done for Him.

I was very aware of my sinfulness and guilt and I was amazed at God's mercy in being willing to save and accept me.

I found that the way up, is down!

How about you?

Do you think God could save you?

The Bible says that God commands '**all men everywhere** to repent'. Do you think that includes you?

It says that 'God so loved the **world** that He gave His only begotten Son that **whoever believes in Him** should not perish but have everlasting life.' Do you think that includes you?

Jesus said 'Come unto Me **all you** who labour and are heavy laden, and I will give you rest'. Do you think that includes you?

God promises that: '**Whoever** calls on the name of the Lord shall be saved'. Do you think that includes you?

Will you?

If you **repent**—say and mean you are very sorry for your sins and that, by God's grace and strength, you will turn from them to Christ—you are included!

If you **believe in** Jesus—put all your confidence for being accepted by God solely in who Jesus is and what He has done for you on the cross and in His resurrection—you are included!

If you **come in prayer**, wherever you are, to Him and ask Him to deal with that burden of sin and guilt and forgive you and cleanse you—you are included!

If you **call on Him now**—you are included.

A prayer

One man in the Bible was so aware of his sins that he dare not even look up but hit himself on the chest and prayed: **'God be merciful to me, a sinner'**.

Jesus assured us that this man was immediately forgiven.

So will you be, if you come with that heart attitude and call upon the Lord Jesus Christ to be merciful and gracious to you, to save you, and to take control of your life as your Lord.

The words you use are far less important than the attitude you have. It might help you, however, to know that my simple prayer was something like this:

'Lord, I am really sorry that I have sinned against You. I know I am guilty and deserve Your punishment for my sins. But thank you that Jesus died on the cross in my place and took my punishment there. Thank you that He rose again and lives today. Please help me now to turn from my sins, and please forgive me , cleanse me from my sins, and come and save me and take control of my life as my Lord'

Further help offered

If your prayer to turn to Christ is
sincere, or if you know you need
Christ to forgive and change you but
have not yet come to Him, or if you
are seriously seeking for God, please
make contact with the church,
organisation or person shown
opposite in order to receive further
help. Meanwhile do read part of the
Bible each day—we suggest you read
daily a chapter of John's gospel—and
ask God to speak to you through it.
He will, if you ask Him!

Bible references

The teaching of this booklet is taken from truths found in the Bible, God's word. The Bible is the king of all books, because it is God's book. Its precious life-changing truths shine and sparkle from it, like the priceless jewels in a royal crown at the world famous Tower of London. You can find some of the basic teaching in the references listed on page 31, and you might like to look up some of them. They follow the order in which their truths are dealt with in this booklet.

(The number before the 'v' refers to the chapter of the book in the Bible, and the number after the 'v' refers to the verse number in that chapter. The books of the Bible are listed in the index at the front of the Bible.) ▶

◁ If you do not possess a Bible, but would like to, please write to the address on page 28 and request one.

The Bible references on page 31 are in blue, and red. Blue references are from the Old Testament, which was written before Jesus came to earth as a baby.

Red references are from the New Testament, which deals with details about Jesus, the church, and the future.

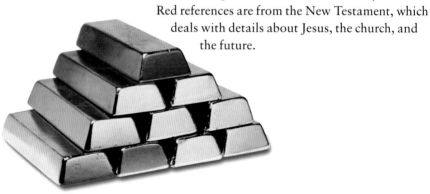

BIBLE REFERENCES

Romans 3v23	Psalm 90v2	Acts 4v12	2 Peter 1v1
Isaiah 53v6	Hebrews 13v8	1 Peter 2v24	Luke 14v11
Exodus 20v1-17	Matthew 5v48	1 Peter 3v18	Acts 17v30
Romans 7v19	Romans 2v16	Isaiah 53v4,5	John 3v16
Romans 7v24	Hebrews 9v27	Mark 10v45	2 Thessalonians 1v7-10
Jeremiah 17v9,10	Proverbs 15v3	1 Timothy 2v6	Matthew 11 v28
Mark 7v21-23	Romans 1v18	Matthew 1v23	Romans 10v13
Leviticus 19v2	Romans 6v23	Hebrews 7v26-28	Acts 3v19
Psalm 145v17	Revelation 20v10-15	Mark 10v21	Acts 16v31
Habbakuk 1v13	Revelation 21v27	Mark 1v29-2v12	Philippians 4v6
Psalm 45v7	Revelation 21v4	1 Corinthians 15v3,4	2 Corinthians 6v2
Zechariah 8v17	Acts 16v30	Acts 1v3	Luke 18v13
1 John 3v4	Proverbs 14v12	1 Thessalonians	
	Ephesians 2v8,9	4v16,17	
	John 14v6	1 John 1v8,9, 12	

KEY: BLUE = OLD TESTAMENT   RED = NEW TESTAMENT

© **Day One** 2000
All rights reserved.

If you require
further copies of
this booklet, please
write for details.

3 Epsom Business Park
Kiln Lane
Epsom
Surrey
KT17 1JF

info@dayone.co.uk

www.dayone.co.uk

Scripture quotations are
from The New King
James Version.

British Library
Cataloguing in
Publication Data
available.

ISBN 1 903087 09 0

DESIGNED BY STEVE DEVANE. PRINTED BY ALDERSON BROTHERS LIMITED, SURREY

ISBN 1 903087 09-0

KI-423-103

DayOne

INTRODUCTION

When Sicilians make the 3-km (2-mile) trip across the Strait of Messina, they are likely to say that they are going to Italy. Italians on the peninsula, for that matter, tend to think of their neighbours in Sicily as foreigners, or at least as being a bit foreign – and this is a distinction with which few Sicilians would take issue.

Travellers will quickly notice that Sicily feels different from any place else either in Italy or in other parts of Europe. To understand why, you need only look to the past. The events of history have left a distinct imprint on Sicily which is in evidence everywhere on the island. Just about all the powers that prowled the Mediterranean over the past 3,000 years set their sights on Sicily, and they left behind many stunning relics of their presence.

The juxtaposition of classical temples, mosaic-filled churches and ornate piazzas lends a theatrical and decidedly unique presence to the island. In Palermo, the cathedral that the Spanish so richly ornamented is only steps away from the mosaic-filled palace that was the seat of the enlightened courts of the island's Saracen and Norman rulers; the Baroque churches and piazzas of Catania incorporate columns of Roman temples; medieval Erice is built near the site of a temple allegedly erected by some of the island's earliest settlers, the Elymians.

Many islanders still speak Sicilian, a combination of words and sounds from the long Greek, Latin, Aragonese, Arabic and Norman-French past; Sicilian is as foreign to an Italian from north of the strait as it is to someone who doesn't speak a word of Italian. The food in Sicily is different from that of

Temple at Selinunte

the mainland, too: the lemons, capers and almonds that the Arabs brought with them from North Africa still appear in many dishes. Since most Sicilians don't live far from the sea, fish, often the *pesce spada* (swordfish) caught in the Strait of Messina, is a staple on most menus.

Sicilian way of life

Travellers will probably notice that Sicilians approach life a little differently than other Italians do. It is difficult to quantify exactly what these differences are, but being among Sicilians is one of the pleasures of touring

Sicilian man in Sunday best

the island. They are welcoming to their visitors, and are likely to strike up a conversation about a son who studied in London or a cousin who lives in Chicago or Brooklyn (almost a third of the island's population emigrated in the late 19th and early 20th century). Afternoon closures, which afford shopkeepers and office workers a chance to enjoy lunch and a nap, are a little longer than they are on the mainland, usually from 1–4pm. Standing patiently in an orderly line is *not* a Sicilian characteristic; finding an occasion to socialise, whether at one of the street markets that are still the mainstay of commerce on the island or at one of the festivals that all towns and cities celebrate at some time during the year, is, and one of which visitors are welcome to partake.

A diverse island

Sicily is the largest island in the Mediterranean, a hefty 25,708 sq km (9,926 square miles), and its landscapes of tall mountains, vast coastal plains and inland valleys are more diverse than those of many countries. The Sicilian scenery is dramatic, sometimes harsh but seldom graceless. The island is also remarkably rich in what can only be described as spectacle. A traveller to Sicily soon notices that the countryside, towns and monuments here are a little more extravagant than they are elsewhere.

Mount Etna, Europe's most forceful volcano, is also Sicily's tallest mountain and most famous natural wonder. It dominates, and periodically threatens, the eastern coast. The Madonie are rugged mountains that rise behind the northern coast, and Capo San Vito, a rocky headland etched with beaches and secluded coves, is at the island's northwestern tip. The volcano on Strómboli, one of the Aeolian Islands that float off the northern coast, can be counted on to provide a round-the-clock performance: it sends fiery lava down the mountainside into the hissing sea about every half hour.

Topping a short and by no means inclusive list of other places to include on even the briefest tour would be Agrigento, Selinunte and Segesta, with the largest and best-preserved Greek temples on the island.

Cefalù, on the northern coast, and Taormina, on the eastern coast, are justifiably the island's most popular seaside resorts. Aside from their beaches, these pleasant towns also throw in some

Outdoor fun

Sicily has increasing appeal for active visitors. Coast, islands and mountains lend themselves to year-round sporting activities, from hiking up mountains and volcanoes to scuba diving and snorkelling in marine reserves, gorge trekking and exploring offshore islands. At a stretch you could even ski on Etna in the morning and sun yourself on the coast in the afternoon.

Trápani fish market

remarkable monuments: a Greek theatre and medieval palaces in Taormina, a Norman cathedral and an Arabic old town in Cefalù. Erice, on the west coast, is the most dramatically poised town on the island, perched atop the rocky escarpment of a tall mountain high above windmill-studded salt pans and the sea.

Ancient cities and towns

Palermo, the capital, is on the northern coast, and Catania, the island's second largest city, is on the eastern coast. Beyond the unattractive modern outskirts of both are old centres filled with monuments that include Norman remnants in Palermo and Baroque churches and piazzas in Catania – both charged with urban vitality. These are, in fact, two of Italy's most fascinating, and often overlooked, cities.

In the southeastern corner of the island is an unusually satisfying collection of cities and towns. Siracusa, the most powerful centre of Greek Sicily, is here, and its ancient ruins lie among an atmospheric Baroque city built by the Bourbons. Just inland, beyond fortifications that the Emperor Dionysius erected around the city, are the Unesco-listed towns designed in the unrestrained style known as the Sicilian Baroque. Of them, Noto takes the prize for architectural fantasy and is a stage set of curving staircases and lavish porticoes. A little deeper into the interior, nestling among oak and hazel woods is the little village of Casale near Piazza Armerina. Here, at the Villa Romana, are some of the most extensive Roman floor mosaics ever uncovered.

Regeneration

Travellers will come to Sicily with some notions of the island's ongoing woes, most notably the activities of the Mafia, or else Cosa Nostra. What is all too apparent is the unregulated building that has fattened Mafia coffers. In cities elsewhere in Italy, modern housing and industrial zones are usually carefully planned so as not to intrude on historic centres and rural landscapes. Cities in Sicily, unfortunately, are often ringed with uncontrolled modern building put up with little regard for the environs. Even the vista of the temples at Agrigento has been partly marred by illegal modern construction.

In recent years, however, the Mafia has begun to lose its grip. A genuine grassroots movement is calling for change and the confiscation of Mafia property continues apace. The refusal to support the Mafia in many quarters is just part of Sicily's revamped image: the Palermitani and Catanese have been busy

Beach at Marza, Ragusa

Monreale cloisters

restoring their churches and palaces, Baroque towns in the southeast have been regenerated and museums re-opened. The government has set aside the Madonie mountains, Lo Zingaró near San Vito Lo Capo and other beautiful landscapes as protected reserves; and the island has seen an increase in the number of chic hotels and *agriturismi* (farm stays).

Sicily's sights

If you want to take in a broad swathe of Sicily's magnificent sights, here are a few suggestions on places to base yourself en route: Palermo is well-situated for exploring the western half of the island and offers good public transport to Monreale, Mondello and places further afield such as Segesta, Cefalù and the Madonie mountains; from Taormina you can easily make excursions to Catania and Mount Etna; Siracusa puts the Baroque towns of the southeast within easy reach; from Agrigento, Piazza Armerina and the Villa Romana mosaics at nearby Casale can be reached by train and bus or by car; and medieval Erice is a beautiful spot from which to explore Marsala, Mozia and the sands of San Vito Lo Capo.

Of course, you'll also want to board a boat in Milazzo for a trip out to the Aeolian islands, or from Trápani to the Egadi islands or Pantelleria. But if you have to press on, don't be too upset: in Sicily, things tend to stay around for a very long time.

A BRIEF HISTORY

All roads may lead to Rome, but for much of recorded history all sea lanes have led to Sicily. The island's position, strategically sited in the middle of the Mediterranean, has been both the proverbial curse and a blessing. Sicilians haven't enjoyed too many centuries of peace, but the various powers that coveted and ruled their island over the centuries left behind a heady mix of cultures and riches.

The Greeks, Romans and Carthaginians turned the island into one of the great battlefields of ancient times; the Normans routed the Saracens, and the Spanish stepped in to replace the French.

The Phoenicians left a remarkable settlement, Mozia, on the little island of San Pantaleo, off the western coast while Sicily's Ancient Greek cities, especially those at Siracusa, Agrigento, Selinunte and Segesta, provide us with some of the best-preserved architectural remnants to come down from the classical age. The sumptuous mosaics at Casale are just some of the many remains of the Romans, who were here until the last days of the Empire; and the Cappella Palatina in Palermo as well as the cathedral at Monreale show off the considerable achievements of the Normans, who came to Sicily from the lands of northern France. The Castello Ursino in Catania is an example of the fortifications required to defend a foothold in Sicily during the Middle Ages.

Early settlers

Long before these empires began to establish strongholds in Sicily, Paleolithic and Neolithic peoples were

The Phoenicians

Ever since the Phoenicians began pulling ashore, sometime around the 8th century BC, many of the powers of the Mediterranean and European world have fought for a stake in Sicily.

Temple of Concord, Valley of the Temples

occupying settlements scattered across the island. By the 10th century BC, a tribe known as the Sicili had migrated from mainland Italy to Sicily, giving the island its name. The Sicili settled in the east; the Sicani, from North Africa, and the Elymians, thought to have descended from the Trojans, established themselves in the west.

Sometime around the 8th century BC, Phoenicians sailed from the shores of the eastern Mediterranean to establish outposts at Mozia and elsewhere in Sicily. The Greeks, who would eventually overpower all these cultures, began arriving about the same time. Most of the Greek settlers came in search of land to farm, and Sicily offered vast tracts of fertile soil and ideal growing conditions. From colonies in Siracusa and elsewhere along the east coast, the Greeks spread across the island, establishing colonies at Gela, Agrigento and Selinunte. Agrigento, known to the ancients as Akragras, became especially powerful, and enough is left of this city on the southern

coast to suggest the extent of its wealth. However, Siracusa soon became the supreme power on Sicily.

The Greek centuries

In 480BC, the armies of the various Greek colonies joined forces under Gelon, the tyrannical ruler of Siracusa, to defeat the Carthaginians at Himera, on Sicily's northern coast. The Greek victory ensured the supremacy of Siracusa in the affairs of Sicily until the city fell to the Romans some 250 years later. The victory also assured that Sicily would become a major Greek power in the Mediterranean; in fact, Sicily and the southern Italian mainland became known as Magna Graecia (Greater Greece) and had a larger Greek population than Greece itself.

Greek dominance, however, didn't bring an end to warfare. The colonies often fought among themselves. Segesta, an Athenian satellite on the northwestern coast, was almost continually at war with Selinunte, an ally of Siracusa on the southern coast. Athens was alarmed by the ambitions of Siracusa and saw an opportunity to attack when Segesta asked for help in repelling the attacks from Selinunte. Athens assembled a massive fleet and sailed to Sicily in 415BC; but the so-called Great Expedition ended in a humiliating defeat for the Athenians. The Siracusans imprisoned some 7,000 Athenian soldiers and put them to work in its limestone quarries, the Latomie.

Carthage, the colony the Phoenicians settled on the north shore of Africa near modern-day Tunis,

Greek tyrants

Although in general usage the word 'tyrant' implies someone oppressive and cruel, in the Ancient world the word existed more as a title which declared a man to be the absolute ruler of a Greek colony, and probably someone who had seized power – not unlike today's dictators. Some tyrants, like Theron, father-in-law of Gelon of Siracusa, were considered wise and fair.

Detail of *Triumph of Death* fresco at Palazzo Abatellis

wasn't as easy to quell. The Carthaginian general Hannibal attacked Selinunte, Agrigento and other Sicilian cities. Siracusa's tyrannical ruler, Dionysius I, retaliated in 397BC by leveling Mozia, the Carthaginian stronghold on the island. Under Agathocles, Sicilian troops crossed the Mediterranean and attacked the Carthaginians on their own turf.

In the 3rd century BC, Sicily became the battleground of the Punic Wars that broke out between Rome and Carthage. When Siracusa sided with the Carthaginians in the Second Punic War, Rome sacked the city in 211BC and took control of the island. The Roman Empire continued to control Sicily for the next seven centuries.

Romans and Saracens

For Rome, Sicily was one vast wheat field, supplying the Empire with grain. For the most part Roman rule brought a commodity that until then was unknown in Sicily – peace, as well as the amphitheatres, baths and other Roman structures that still stand around the island.

Christianity arrived in Sicily around AD200, and Siracusa became one of the most fervent early Christian strongholds in the Mediterranean, thousands of Siracusans worshipping

and burying their dead in catacombs beneath the city until the Emperor Constantine lifted the prohibition against Christians a century later. Not long after Rome fell to the Visigoths in 410, Sicily became prey to Vandals and Ostrogoths who sacked the coasts. By 535 the island had fallen into the hands of the Byzantines; Siracusa was capital of the Eastern Byzantine Empire for five years, from 663 to 668.

The next wave of invasion came from North Africa. The island of Pantelleria, where an Arabic influence is still much in evidence, fell first in 700. It wasn't until the 9th century that the assault began in force. After decades of fighting, the so-called Saracens – including Arabs, Spanish Muslims and Berbers – took Palermo in 831 and Siracusa in 878. Arab rule ushered in another golden age for Sicily. Palermo became one of the largest and most cosmopolitan cities in the world, comparable to Constantinople and Baghdad. The Muslim rulers revitalised the countryside, building irrigation systems and introducing oranges and lemons to the landscape.

Once again, the prosperity of Sicily proved to be irresistible to other powers. This time it was a Norman lord, Roger de Hauteville, who set his sights on the island and took Messina in 1061. All of Sicily was under Norman rule by 1091, with Palermo as its capital and Roger as its ruler. Rather than impose a foreign yoke on the island, Roger accommodated the island's rich Greek, Roman, Byzantine and Roman heritage – Norman art and architecture, so richly preserved in the Norman churches in Palermo, Monreale and Cefalù, displays this fusion. When Roger's son was crowned Roger II, King of Sicily, in 1130, his holdings included Sicily and most of southern Italy and his court was one of the wealthiest and most cosmopolitan in the world.

Stupor Mundi and the Sicilian Vespers

A descendant, Frederick II von Hohenstaufen, was to carry on the Norman tradition of enlightened rule when he took the

Castle in Erice

crown in 1220. His mother was Catherine, Roger II's daughter, and his father was Henry VI of Swabia; this heritage gave him control of Sicily, much of Italy and parts of Germany. He introduced a unified legal system, promoted the arts and sciences and encouraged a blending of Islamic, Jewish and Christian cultures. Frederick ruled for more than 40 years and became known as *Stupor Mundi*, the Wonder of the World.

Frederick's death once again left Sicily up for grabs. Among the contenders was the Papacy under Pope Urban IV, eager to get control of the lands of southern Italy. Backed by the Pope, Charles of Anjou, brother of the French King Saint Louis, defeated the Hohenstaufen supporters in a series of battles and became King of Sicily and Naples in 1268. Determined to punish Sicily for its loyalty to the Hohenstaufens, Charles imposed heavy taxes and confiscated lands.

An uprising against French rule broke out in Palermo on 30 March 1282; the first shots rang out at the hour the bells of the church of Santo Spirito rang for Vespers, and the revolt has come to be known as the Sicilian Vespers. Some scholars claim that it was instigated by the Byzantine Emperor Michael VIII, who had learned that Charles was plotting to attack Constantinople and wrest control of Byzantine lands, and wished to divert the French by keeping them busy in Sicily. The immediate cause was an incident in which a French soldier stopped a Sicilian bride on her way to church and searched her for concealed weapons. An angry crowd killed the soldier immediately, and within days the citizenry had slaughtered more than 8,000 French troops across the island.

King Peter III of Aragón (whose wife, Constance, was a Hohenstaufen) arrived in a flotilla five months later, and the Sicilian nobles offered the Spaniard the throne. The Angevins and the Aragonese skirmished for control of the island for the next 20 years, and in the end Sicily belonged to the Spanish – and would remain in their hands for the next 400 years.

Masters of a Sicilian Style

While the achievements of Greeks and Normans are often what capture a visitor's attention, Sicilian artists have made considerable contributions of their own – several artists developed a distinctly Sicilian style in their work. You will encounter them frequently around the island.

Domenico Gagini (1448–1492) came to Palermo in 1458 and spent the rest of his life gracing churches with his elegant Madonnas and other sculptures; his son, **Antonello** (1478–1536), carried on the tradition by becoming Sicily's foremost sculptor of the Renaissance. You will find their work in numerous churches and in Palermo's Galleria Regionale della Sicilia, where a room is filled with Gagini masterpieces.

Rosario Gagliardi (1700–1770) is the architect who created many of the Baroque churches and public buildings that transform towns like Noto and Ragusa into stage sets. The church of San Giorgio in Ragusa is a fine example of his mastery of this whimsical style.

Antonello da Messina (1430–1479) combined a mastery of light and spatial depth to create such masterpieces as his *Portrait of an Unknown Man*, now in the Museo Mandralisca in Cefalù.

Giacomo Serpotta (1656–1732) perfected the art of stucco work, or moulded plaster. His creations, which adorn the Oratorio del Rosario di San Domenico and other oratorios in Palermo, cover the walls with delicate religious imagery.

Puppet shows in Sicily date back centuries

Spanish rule

Sicily became more or less a backwater when the European powers directed their expansionist ambitions to the New World. This inattention ensured that Sicily enjoyed one of the few periods of long peace in its history. In the absence of human drama, nature stepped in. The plague, brought to Sicily by the ships that called at its harbours, broke out repeatedly and decimated large portions of the population.

The end of the 17th century was especially calamitous. Mount Etna erupted in 1669 and sent molten lava flowing through the streets of Catania. An earthquake in 1693, also centred in the east, was even more destructive and took an enormous toll on human life. Sicilians rebuilt Noto and other cities in a distinctive style, the Sicilian Baroque.

The Treaty of Utrecht divided Spanish holdings, and in the early 18th century Sicily once again became a pawn of foreign powers. The island passed from the Italian House of Savoy to the Austrians and, in 1734, back to the Spanish, this time to the Bourbons. The British convinced the Bourbon king Ferdinand I to introduce a constitution, but he soon repealed it and called in Austrian mercenaries when citizens took to the streets of Palermo and other cities calling for independence;

his successor, Ferdinand II, bombarded Messina in 1848 to quell an uprising for independence there.

From unification into the present

This unrest set the stage for Giuseppe Garibaldi, leader of the Risorgimento, the campaign for the unification of Italy. He sailed into Marsala on 11 May 1860 with his so-called Thousand, a reference to the guerrilla army that accompanied him. Garibaldi's soldiers and Sicilian partisans were soon fighting in Palermo, and the island was free of Bourbon rule within a year. Sicilians were soon disillusioned – widespread poverty and government repression made life as part of a unified Italy more difficult than it had been under the Bourbons.

For many Sicilians, the only escape from impoverishment was emigration. By 1914, more than a million and a half Sicilians had left the island, usually for North and South America. The reforms introduced later by Mussolini and his fascist government did little to alleviate poverty, illiteracy and unemployment in Sicily.

The island once again became a battleground in World War II. In July 1943, the Allies made their first European landings at Gela on the southern coast while British and Canadian forces tackled the east coast. Allied bombardments flattened Messina, where the German defensive was entrenched. Other cities were not spared. In fact, parts of Palermo are still strewn with rubble from World War II bombings,

Origins of the Mafia

The Mafia took root in Sicily in the 1860s, ostensibly to help the rural poor have their share of the land reform and other benefits that were to accompany freedom from rule. In effect, the Mafia became an integral part of the island's power structure, controlling business and the workings of government, and today is said to ensure that Sicily remains a centre for drug trafficking.

Bustling centre of Catania

largely because government funds for rebuilding were misappropriated by corrupt officials who were linked with the Mafia.

In the early 1980s, a Mafia war left Palermo's streets strewn with blood and the Corleone-based clan the undisputed victors. In 1992 two anti-Mafia magistrates were murdered. The terror continued with bombs in Milan and Rome that killed bystanders. The revulsion sparked in Sicilians by these assassinations has since weakened the Mafia's grip on public opinion and dented the age-old code of loyalty (*omertà*). A grassroots association (Addiopizzo) was set up to fight against the payment of the *pizzo*, protection money, and since it was founded hundreds of businesses across Sicily have signed up.

No one could pretend however that Costa Nostra has disappeared. Its influence is still shaping politics and it is more often than not seen as the cause of Sicily's economic stagnation. In 2013 the island has a debt pile of over €6 billion, which is endangering Italy's already frail financial state. Sicily's economy is based on public sector wages: there are 144,000 public sector employees among a population of 5 million, mostly underused and employed on the traditional jobs-for-votes exchange. Unemployment is at nearly 20 per cent, twice the national average. On the positive side, tourism is on the up, with an increasing number of visitors to the island, attracted by vastly improved accommodation, rural and island retreats, restored sites and rejuvenated historic centres.

Historical Highlights

Before 10,000BC Paleolithic and Neolithic peoples settle in the Egadi Islands.

10th century BC Sicili, Sicani and Elymians settle in Sicily.

8th century BC Phoenicians establish outposts at Mozia; Greek colonists settle in Gela, Agrigento and Selinunte.

480BC The Greeks defeat the Carthaginians. Siracusa becomes Sicily's most powerful city.

211BC Following Second Punic War, Rome takes control of Sicily.

c.200AD Early Christianity takes hold in Sicily.

663–668 Siracusa now capital of eastern Byzantine Empire.

9th century Saracens take Palermo and Siracusa to rule Sicily.

11th century Roger de Hauteville brings Sicily under Norman rule.

1220 Frederick II von Hohenstaufen, of Norman and Swabian heritage, takes the crown and brings 40 years of enlightened rule to Sicily.

1268 Charles of Anjou becomes King of Sicily and Naples.

30 March 1282 The Sicilian Vespers uprising ousts the French and installs the Spanish.

1693 An earthquake flattens cities in the southeast; in rebuilding, the flamboyant style of Sicilian Baroque is created.

1734 Sicily passes to the Spanish house of Bourbon.

11 May 1860 Giuseppe Garibaldi sails into Marsala; Sicilians oust the Bourbons to become part of the new Kingdom of Italy.

Late 19th–early 20th centuries Many Sicilians emigrate.

July 1943 Allies make first European landings of World War II in Sicily.

1951-1975 One million Sicilians emigrate.

1980s–1990s Mafia violence triggers government crackdown and citizen movements against organized crime.

2006 Mafia boss Bernardo Provenzano arrested after years in hiding.

2011 Italian 'technocratic' government replaces Silvio Berlusconi. 20,000 Tunisians arrive on the Sicilian island of Lampedusa.

2013 New airport expected to open at Comiso.

WHERE TO GO

The easiest way to see a good measure of Sicily's cities, ruins, beaches and other attractions is to circle the coast and make occasional forays into the interior and to nearby islands. We begin in Palermo, and head east to start a tour.

PALERMO

Palermo ❶ does not readily enchant its visitors. The chaotic capital of Sicily is noisy and traffic-filled, riddled with decay in parts, overbuilt with concrete in others. But take your time and walk the narrow streets and alleys of the old city. You'll discover Norman palaces, Baroque churches, chapels shimmering in mosaics, outdoor markets overflowing with olives and blood oranges, quaint puppet theatres and grandiose oratories; and, smoothing out the rough edges, a great deal of warm-hearted street life. Moreover the city is being revitalized, with the restoration of some of the major churches and museums and the opening of new contemporary galleries.

The Quattro Canti

The **Quattro Canti Ⓐ**, or Four Corners, is the hectic crossroads at the centre of the old city that divides it into four *quartiere*, quarters; most of Palermo's sights are an easy walk from this busy junction, the intersection of the Via Maqueda and the Corso Vittorio Emanuele. The façades of the buildings on each corner here – three Baroque palazzi and the church of **San Giuseppe dei Teatini** – are ornamented with fountains, and each is also embellished in turn with statuary that represents a season, one of four Spanish kings of Sicily and the patron saint of one of the

Ragusa Ibla

four quarters that surround the Quattro Canti. If the church is open, step inside for a look at the angels, stuccoes, frescoes and other ornamentation that are typical of the Sicilian Baroque.

Piazza Pretoria  **B** is just a few steps south along Via Maqueda. The **Fontana Pretoria** takes up most of the square and in more puritan times was nicknamed the Piazza della Vergogna, or Square of Shame – this being a reference to the seeming licentiousness of the naked figures who frolic in the spray. More than 30 naked or near-naked nymphs, tritons, gods and youths of varying sizes and quality surround the fountain's vast circular basin. Garibaldi is said to have sat on the edge of the fountain during the fierce battles of 1870, instilling the citizenry with the courage to fight on for independence. Flanking one side of the square is the **Palazzo delle Aquile**, the town hall, named for the stone eagles that decorate its façade. The other massive presence is the church of **Santa Caterina**; behind its austere façade is another Baroque interior, covered with brightly coloured frescoes and plasterwork angels that tumble from every surface.

In Piazza Pretoria, Palermo

The Piazza Bellini, just a few steps to the east, is graced with the three small red domes of the chapel of **San Cataldo** **C** (open Mon–Sat 9am–2pm, 3.30–7pm, Sun 9am–2pm) and the 12th-century campanile of **La**

Martorana D. San Cataldo is squat and plain, and aside from its mosaic flooring, was left undecorated when its founder, a chancellor of William I, died in 1160. La Martorana (closed for restoration) is more elaborate, and was founded by George of Antioch, Roger II's chief min-

ister, in 1146 as a seat of the Greek Orthodox church. Despite a Baroque restoration that added the cupids around the entryway, much of the Norman mosaic work remains intact. The gold, green and azure tiles of the dome depict Christ flanked by saints and prophets, and a nearby mosaic of Christ crowning Roger II is said to be a reliable likeness of the Norman king.

The Albergheria

The streets and alleys of the Albergheria quarter, once the home of Norman court officials and rich merchants from Pisa and Amalfi, stretch south and west of Piazza Bellini. Via Maqueda and Via Bosco lead into the centre of the quarter, the Piazza Carmine, passing stately palaces, centuries-old buildings that show their age and the occasional rubble-filled site left by World War II bombings. The stalls of the **Mercato di Ballarò E**, Palermo's liveliest daily market, fill Piazza Carmine, the adjacent Piazza Ballarò and the surrounding streets. It is raucous, sprawling and exotic, with mountains of lemons and oranges, slabs of tuna and swordfish, pigs' trotters and intestines. Above this busy scene rises the green-and-white dome of **Chiesa del Gesù**, founded in the late 16th century as the first Jesuit church in Sicily, and that of the church of the **Carmine**. While the interior of Il Gesù is another swirl of Baroque excess, that of the Carmine is vast and far more sedate.

Palermo's Cathedral

The Cattedrale and Palazzo dei Normanni

From Quattro Canti, Corso Vittorio Emanuele leads west past shops and Baroque palaces to several of Palermo's most important monuments. The first is the **Cattedrale** 🅕 (Mon–Sat 7am–7pm, Sun 8am–1pm and 4–7pm) that was begun in 1185 but not completed, with the addition of a dome, until 1801. As a result, the building is an incongruous mixture of styles: the 12th-century towers are Norman, the façade and south porch are Gothic and the interior is coldly Neoclassical.

The church is a pantheon of the Normans, who came to Sicily in 1061, routed the Arabs and ruled the island ably for a century. Roger II, the Norman king who made the island the centre of the Mediterranean World, was interred here among his royal relations against his will: he wanted to be buried in the cathedral he built in Cefalù (see page 44). In the adjacent Treasury, Constance of Aragon's bejeweled crown is on display alongside rings and other artifacts removed from the royal

tombs during a 19th-century rearrangement. Of a more maca-
bre nature are the relics of several saints, including a withered
extremity said to be the foot of Mary Magdalen.

A short distance away is the **Palazzo dei Normanni**, or
Palazzo Reale, that actually was built by Sicily's Arab rulers
in the ninth century. Under both the Arabs and the Normans,
Palermo was one of the largest and most civilised cities in the
world and the palace was a centre of the arts and learning.

Little of the Arab and Norman palace remains: the façade
that overlooks the old city is a 17th-century addition made by
the island's Spanish rulers, and many of the salons and lesser
quarters are now occupied by Sicily's regional government. One
stunning Norman remnant, however, is the **Cappella Palatina**
Ⓖ (open Mon–Sat 8.30am–5pm, Sun 8.15am–12.15pm but
no visits 9.45am–11am when religious celebrations take place;
charge), the exquisite chapel commissioned by Roger II. Mosaics
cover every surface, depicting the tales of the Old and New
Testaments in a frank, charming style that infuses the softly lit
space with a sense of faith and earnest artistry executed for the
love of God and a just ruler. Capping the glittering profusion of
gold and silver tiles is a purely
Arab touch: a honeycombed,
wooden ceiling.

A marble staircase leads
from the chapel to the Royal
Apartments (guided tours
Fri–Mon only, 8.30am–
5.30pm; charge). The best
room, in a small wing of the
original Norman palace, is
the Sala di Re Ruggero. The
walls are covered in mosaics
of hunting scenes and exotic
landscapes.

Glittering mosaics in the
Palatine Chapel

Oratorio di Santa Cita

San Giovanni degli Eremiti

Another remnant of Norman Palermo, the now deconsecrated church of **San Giovanni degli Eremiti**  (open daily 9am–6pm; charge) sits just south of the palace on Via dei Benedittini. While the interior is stark and devoid of elaborate decoration, this five-domed Norman-Arab church is beautiful in its simplicity and is surrounded by gardens and cloisters planted with palms, cactus and jasmine. The **Parco d'Orleans** across the street is named for the one-time resident of the palace it surrounds: Louis-Philippe d'Orléans, who was exiled here in 1809 in the aftermath of the Paris Commune and later returned to France to become King. The palace is now the residence of the Regional President.

From the Vucciria to Piazza Verdi

Corso Vittorio Emanuele leads northeast from Quattro Canti towards the sea and several other quarters of old Palermo. Just a few blocks from the Quattro Canti, the Corso crosses Via Roma, which slightly north skirts the **Vucciria** ❶ market. Steps descend into a warren of stalls, from which you might emerge with a religious medallion or two and bags filled with the capers, olives, lemons and other produce that grows in such abundance across Sicily.

A few blocks north of the market, Via Roma comes to **Piazza San Domenico**, an airy square dominated by the

containing the grave of the saint. The impressive silver coffin was made in 1829 by Diamantis Bafas. He also made the silver surrounds for the icons on the church's intricately carved wooden iconostasis. The saint has two festival days, celebrated on 24 August and 17 December.

Bóhali Froúrio

Above the town in the Bóhali district, is the huge Venetian **Froúrio** ⓓ, or fort (daily 8am–2.30pm; charge). Thought to stand on the site of ancient Psophida, the fortress has Byzantine antecedents, but any traces of these earlier settlements – with the exception of the 12th-century church of the Pandokrátor – have been destroyed by earthquakes. The present fortifications were built under the Venetian *Proveditor general da mar* Giovanni Battisto Grimani and finished in 1646. As a prime defensive site, the fort served as a place of refuge

The Froúrio walls

for local people and, particularly in the 17th century, became a flourishing settlement. The fort fell into disuse in 1864, when Zákynthos became part of the Greek Republic.

The Froúrio lies at the end of a winding road that leads up from the town through Bóhali village. Just before the top of the hill is the village *platía* in front of the church, with a few cafés and tavernas that have a lovely view over Zákynthos Town and harbour. The inside of the fort is now a beautiful pine wood, and you have to search around for the remains of the buildings (there is a useful site plan at the entrance). However, perhaps the main reason for coming up to the Froúrio is the spectacular panoramic view. The site's slow renovation by the EU and Greek Ministry of Culture has ground to a halt and shorter opening hours mean sunsets

Sonnet – To Zante

Fair isle, that from the fairest of all flowers,
Thy gentlest of all gentle names dost take!
How many memories of what radiant hours
At sight of thee and thine at once awake!
How many scenes of what departed bliss!
How many thoughts of what entombéd hopes!
How many visions of a maiden that is
No more – no more upon thy verdant slopes!
No more! Alas, that magical sad sound
Transforming all! Thy charms shall please no more –
Thy memory no more! Accurséd ground
Henceforth I hold thy flower-enamelled shore,
O hyacinthine isle! O purple Zante!
'Isola d'oro! Fior di Levante!'

Edgar Allan Poe, 1837

must be enjoyed from the cafés below.

On the way up Bóhali hill, on the left-hand side coming from town, is the **Zákynthos Nautical Museum** (daily 9am–2pm, 6–9pm; charge). The work of one man, the museum tells the history of Greek seafaring through a series of model boats, as well as an eclectic assortment of naval artefacts.

Vines are intensively cultivated in these parts

CENTRAL PLAIN

The island's central plain is the most fertile in the Ionian Islands. It is mostly given over to the intensive cultivation of vines and, away from the resorts and airport, is sprinkled with attractive little villages. Separating the plain from the eastern coast is a line of steep but low hills, and on the western side the mountains rise sharply and dramatically. Along the foot of mountains lie a string of villages, many located at points where springs emerge from the hills above.

The central villages include sleepy little Gaïtáni with an attractive Italianate church, and a characteristic separate bell tower, which dates from 1906. Similar architecture can be seen in neighbouring tiny settlements of Vanáto and Hourhoulídi. The detached bell towers seen across the island are built away from the church to prevent the bells falling through its roof in the event of an earthquake.

On the road between Zákynthos Town and Maherádo is the **Ktíma Agría Komoútou** (daily 9am–1pm, 5pm–8pm; free). There has been a vineyard belonging to the Komoútou family

on this spot since 1638 but it was the present owner's father who established the commercial winery, which now produces some of the best wines on the island. You can watch the production of the wines, as well as taste and buy them. Much of the cultivation is organic and there is also good olive oil for sale.

Caper *(káppari)* buds and flowers

Maherádo, Agía Marína and Pigadákia

At the foot of the steep climb up to Kiliómeno is the large village of **Maherádo**, home to a couple of interesting churches and some surviving, albeit decaying, examples of traditional pre-earthquake architecture. The village square by the church of Agías Mávras has two nearby cafés serving basic food such as *souvláki*, salad and *tzatzíki*.

The main sight in Maherádo was the pilgrimage church of **Agías Mávras**. The icon of Agía Mávra was supposedly found on this spot and a church built around it. However, a devastating fire in 2005 destroyed the roof and much of the baroque interior by Nikolaos Latsis. Some of the contents were saved and it is still in the process of being restored. The festival of Agía Mávra, who is said to help healing, is celebrated at the beginning of June.

On the left-hand side, just after turning up the hill towards Kiliómeno, is a modern convent whose church has an attractively painted interior. Wrap-around skirts are provided for visitors whose dress is not modest enough for a church visit.

North of Maherádo, and higher up the mountainside, is the village of **Agía Marína**. The eponymous church has an impressive interior but is often locked. Also here is the **Hélmi Museum of Natural History** (May–Oct daily 9am–6pm, Nov–Apr 9am–2pm; charge), with a small but informative display on the flora and fauna of the island.

Further on is **Pigadákia ❷**, named after its springs (*pigí* in Greek). The lovely 16th-century church of **Agíou Pandelímona** has a holy spring in the saint's shrine under the altar, said to promote healing; this is one of the few places where you can go behind the iconostasis. The traditional *papadosiakoús* dance is performed at the saint's festival on 27 July. The **Vertzagio Museum** (Mar–Nov daily 9am–2pm, Sun–Fri 6–8pm; charge) here has a motley display of rural artefacts.

Gerakári, Kypséli and Tragáki

Three pretty hilltop villages sit on the slopes in the north of the plain. They are **Gerakári**, **Kypséli** and **Tragáki**, the southernmost, largest and most strung out. They all give splendid views over the plain below. One of the few places to eat, with basic food, is Harry's *kafenío* and *psistaría* in Tragáki.

Just north of tiny Limodaíka (near Tragáki) is the **Théatro Avoúri/Skaliá Cultural Centre ❸** (tel: 26950 62973). Established by local actor and storyteller Dimitris Avouris in 1995, the beautiful site has three

View from Gerakári church

stone-built outdoor theatres, which hold from 60 to 1,000 people, as well as a new indoor auditorium. There are storytelling performances four times a week and, as well as holding Greek and pan-European storytelling festivals, the theatre played its part in the 2004 Cultural Olympiad by hosting global storytelling events.

The East Coast

Leaving Zákynthos Town heading north, you pass through **Kryonéri**, along the seafront. The water is reasonably clean, especially given its proximity to the harbour, and the locals swim off the rocks and narrow pebbly beach here. After the steep climb up to pleasant, strung-out Akrotíri, the road runs inland along the ridge before descending back down to the sea at **Tsiliví**. This is the first of a string of resorts and not the most pleasant. Situated on a lovely bay with a decent beach, Tsiliví is dominated by loud bars, shops peddling tourist souvenirs and holidaymakers going red in the sun. Tsiliví blends seamlessly into Plános before things quieten down a bit at Boúka.

After the small promontory of Akrotírio Gáidaros, for the next 4km (2.5 miles) between Aboúla and Amoúdi, the road passes turn-offs to a string of small, quiet beaches. There are rooms to rent at most of them, and there are a couple of excellent beachside tavernas. About 1km (0.6 miles) beyond Amoúdi is **Alikaná**, perhaps the most pleasant of the resorts along this coast. Towards the sea it is still fairly quiet and the mountain backdrop is lovely.

At the northernmost point of the Central Plain is the large resort of **Alykés**. A larger version of Tsiliví, Alykés has all the facilities expected of a Greek package resort – cheap accommodation, all-day English breakfasts and football on satellite TV. It is, however, on a sweeping bay with a sandy beach and views of Kefaloniá. The exposed bay attracts windsurfers and can produce some surf. This is also one of places you can take a boat to the Blue Caves near Skinári (trips are advertised everywhere; see page 49). Behind the town are the old salt-works, the large pans forming shallow lakes where salt was obtained from seawater through evaporation. These are now no longer used, as it is cheaper to import salt from the main-land. Consequently, the stagnant water can be rather smelly.

LAGANÁS BAY

If you dislike mass tourism and loud nightclubs, the place you will most want to avoid on Zákynthos is **Laganás**. Ironically, this, the island's most notorious resort, is right in the mid-dle of its most environmentally sensitive area. It is estimated that Zákynthos receives up to 700,000 visitors every year, half of whom stay in Laganás on the south coast. They come for the wonderful sandy beach that stretches from the Vasilikós

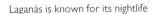

Laganás is known for its nightlife

Peninsula in the east to Límni Kerioú beach in the west. This lively nightspot – or den of iniquity, depending on your point of view – is brash, noisy and nocturnal. Apart from its crowded beach, the resort's main attraction is its nightlife; one of the more popular spots is on the island of Ágios Sóstis, joined to the shore by a walkway. **Kalamáki**, 4km (2.5 miles) east of Laganás, is perhaps the most pleasant of the hectic resorts on this side of the bay.

National Marine Park

In response to these conflicting demands on the bay – and after intense campaigning by local environmentalists – in

National Park Rules

Within the confines of the National Park, you must not:
• fish
• light a fire
• camp
• pick any plants
• throw away ANY rubbish
On turtle nesting beaches there is:
• no access between sunset and sunrise
• no use of umbrellas 5m (16ft) from the waterline
• no digging in the sand
• no disturbing the cages protecting the nests
• no use of any vehicle
• no access to horses
• no access to dogs without a leash
• no use of ANY lights at night
    Access and speed is restricted for boats across the whole area. The strictly protected area around Sekánia has access only for scientists with permission.

1999 the Greek government established the **National Marine Park of Zákynthos** ❹, the country's first. The protected area takes in: the marine area and beaches of Laganás Bay, and around capes Marathiá and Yérakas at either end; an area of land stretching back from the beach, and behind that a buffer zone that extends almost as far as Zákynthos

The National Park logo

Town; and the Strofádes Islands 80km (50 miles) to the south. The park's effectiveness has periodically been compromised due to frequent funding shortages that often leave it unstaffed and unprotected. Thankfully the crusading Gérakas Turtle Information Centre (see page 43) monitors the situation.

However, the entire bay is the most important nesting site for the loggerhead turtle *(Caretta caretta)* in the Mediterranean basin. The turtles are very sensitive to human disturbance and have suffered greatly from the indiscriminate development of this coast.

The turtles roam throughout the Mediterranean (there is evidence to suggest they use the Gulf of Gabés off Tunisia as a wintering ground) and in the spring return to Laganás Bay to nest. They rest and mate in the bay while waiting to come ashore during the night. After nightfall, the females crawl up the beach to find a suitable nesting site in the soft sand; if they are disturbed by noises or lights they will return to the sea without laying any eggs. If they are not disturbed, they dig a deep hole and lay a clutch of about 120 eggs. These take about two months to hatch, after which the hatchlings dig their way to surface and – at night – make their way down to the sea.

Conflicts with humans arise not only due to pressures of space, forcing the turtles on to fewer beaches and raising the nesting density, but particularly due to disturbance of the nests themselves and, once the turtles have emerged from their shells, from light pollution. The hatchlings find their way to the sea using reflected starlight on the water. Any shoreside lighting confuses the tiny turtles, causing them to make their way inland, where they die.

The park is home not only to the famous turtles but also the critically endangered Mediterranean monk seal (11–12 of which inhabit sea caves outside of the park), and is important as a rest stop for migrating birds. It also protects certain species of plants, particularly the sea daffodil (*Pancratium maritimum*) and the seabed cover of Posidonia (*Posidonia oceania*), which contributes a large part of the oxygen in the Mediterranean. The habitat of **Lake Kerí** (Límni Kerioú) is the last remaining wetland of Zákynthos, important for migrating bird species. There used to be a huge lake behind Laganás that stretched almost as far as Zákynthos Town, but this was drained in an act of environmental vandalism to make way for the airport.

The Vasilikós Peninsula

On the eastern side of Laganás Bay is one of the most beautiful parts of the island, the **Vasilikós Peninsula**. Heading south from Zákynthos Town the first place you come to is the resort of Argási, which has suffered more than most places from the tourism decline. As the land starts to rise, things begin to improve. Set against the backdrop of Mount Skopós, there are a string of beautiful small beaches along the northern edge of the peninsula. The longest of these, Paralía Iónio, is near the strung-out village of Vasilikós. Iónio runs into the nudist Banana Beach, and around the cape from here is the popular water sports centre at **Ágios Nikoláos**. On the opposite side of the bay is the unsympathetic development at Pórto Róma.

The best beach, however, is on the southwestern side at **Gérakas** ❺, a superb sweep of sand fringed by cliffs. There is only one problem – this corner of paradise is an important nesting site for turtles. Access is controlled by a park ranger en route to the beach, and numbers are limited to protect the nests. For those who want to get even closer to nature, the far end of the beach is nudist.

The exemplary **Gérakas Turtle Information Centre**, run by the environmental organisation Earth, Sea and Sky, provides information on the turtles and the other flora and fauna of the peninsula. They can also advise on joining volunteer environmental protection programmes (see page 88).

Gérakas beach, where turtle nests are protected

Further back up the peninsula's west coast is the isolated beach of Dáfni, with a pleasant *psarotavérna*, reached by a very rough road from Vasilikós. Between Dáfni and Kalamaki is the totally protected beach of Sekánia (access is only given to scientists with prior permission).

THE HILL VILLAGES AND WEST COAST

The wild and mountainous west coast is the least-spoilt part of the island, with hillsides covered in bright green *maquis*

The cliffs at Cape Kerí

and small, dry-stone-walled fields. The land falls to the sea in precipitous cliffs, with no easily accessible beaches; one reason why it has so far resisted tourist development. The sea caves at the foot of the cliffs are used for breeding by the very few remaining pairs of Mediterranean monk seals *(Monarchus monarchus)*. This, and the so-far near-pristine environment, are the reasons why environmentalists are lobbying for protected status (like that for Laganás Bay) for this region.

The hill villages retain much of their traditional architecture and character. Many pre-earthquake buildings survive, though most are too dangerous to live in. One factor that has contributed to their preservation is that no-one can use the damaged buildings unless they have the permission of the owners.

Kerí and Agalás

On the western side of the southern cape – best crossed by the spectacular but rough road from Marathiá – is the pretty village of **Kerí** ❻. Many of the traditional houses here have been bought up by German and British visitors, giving the village quite a different, and more reserved, character from other places on the island. As well as a 17th-century church, Kerí is known for the *píssa tou Keríou*, or natural tar pools, mentioned by both Herodotus and Pliny. Now dried up, they were previously used for caulking boats. A couple of kilometres down the road is the lighthouse at Cape Kerí.

The minor road north from the village runs through a very attractive wooded valley. It leads to the quiet village of **Agalás**, tucked away in the southwestern part of the island. Next to the church in the centre is the small maritime and natural history museum and art gallery, though, with its erratic opening times you may have to ask around for the key. Further south into the village, at the point where the KTEL buses drop off and pick up, you'll find a café and taverna. Signposted off from the village are some Venetian wells and the Damiános cave; both down towards the sea.

Kilioméno and Loúha

At the top of the long, steep climb from Maherádo (see page 36) is **Kilioméno** ❼. On the right-hand side, just before the road turns for Ágios Léon, is Korfiatos, a wooden balcony with lovely views, where you can have a drink or simple meal. Behind the benches, which seem more Bavarian than Greek, are huge barrels of local wine. As well as the wine there is also excellent local olive oil and thyme honey for sale. Opposite is Kilioméno's rather odd-looking church of Ágios Nikólaos, with its still-unfinished bell tower.

Venetian ruins

One notable feature of the landscape is the ruined stone towers on the tops of the hills. These are the remains of Venetian windmills, previously used for pumping water up from wells.

Loúha village

Leaving Kilioméno, the road turns sharp right and leads to the friendly, if a little lacklustre, village of Ágios Léon. Look out for the Venetian windmill converted into a church tower. A road heading inland from here goes up to **Loúha** ❽, one of the highest, and certainly one of the prettiest, settlements on Zákynthos. The domestic architecture of the hill villages differs from that of the rest of the island; plain exteriors hide pretty courtyards, usually full of flowers, with the living quarters set around them. To get a better look at this arrangement pay a visit to Loúha's tiny village shop and post office (opposite the church of Ioánnis Theológos). The courtyard behind, with a 400-year-old floor, has an attractive taverna on the first floor (with the added bonus of excellent toilets). The previously equally attractive village of Gýrio, just beyond Loúha, has been rather spoilt by a breeze-block factory.

The majority of Zákynthos's high mountain villages are controlled by the KKE (Greek communist party). The communists have organised collective agricultural cooperatives to help local farmers buy machinery, and then harvest and market their produce

From Ágios Léon a pretty but winding, and initially very narrow, road leads down to **Limniónas** by the sea. All that is here is a taverna that looks out over a beautiful rocky bay. Beside the taverna a flight of steps leads down to a small bathing platform.

Éxo Hóra to Anafonítria

The main road carries on north to **Éxo Hóra**. At the crossroads at the village centre is a huge olive tree, reputedly the oldest on the island. The crossroads is also the turn-off for **Kambí**, where a large concrete cross glowers down on the sea from a tall headland. The cross commemorates the place where right-wing soldiers threw a group of local communists to their death in the war, or vice versa, depending whose version of the story you believe.

The unspoilt village of **Mariés** lies further north. Local legend claims Mary Magdalena landed here on her way to or from Rome. This accounts for what seems to be a disproportionate number of churches for the village's size, and for its name (derived from María).

Where the road turns east towards the village of Orthoniés, there is a turn left for **Anafonítria** ❾. Ágios Dionýsios was abbot at the 14th-century monastery here from 1578 to his death in 1622. Further on, above the turn for Navágio, is the 16th-century monastery of **Ágios Geórgios ton Krimnón**, with its striking round tower.

Navágio Bay

Just beyond Anafonítria is the headland overlooking **Navágio Bay** (Shipwreck Bay) ❿, on which is the most photographed beach in the Ionians – a sheltered bay where a rusty freighter lies half-buried in sand. The locals take great exception to the disfigurement of their spectacular beach (it was previously known as Paradise Beach) and decry the fact that the boat is now regarded as a tourist icon – it was scuttled by an unscrupulous captain, allegedly a smuggler, for a fraudulent insurance claim.

However, looking down the sheer cliffs from the small steel-viewing platform above is quite spectacular and, for anyone with even a mild distrust of heights, quite stomach churning. Boat trips shuttle sightseers to the beach from **Pórto Vrómi**, below Mariés. The bigger operators are perhaps best avoided for environmental reasons; boats above a certain size are not supposed to land on the beach, but they invariably do.

Back on the main road, heading further north brings you to Volímes (see page 49).

THE NORTH

North of Alykés the landscape becomes more desolate, rugged and deserted. It was this part of the island that felt the

The Blue Caves

flat beaches, with volcanic black sand to the north of the jetty, stone and shingley sand to the south.

Among the other small islands, pretty **Panarea**  is where rich Italians and celebrities have summer homes, while **Filicudi** and **Alicudi** are prized for their quiet and only come to life in the holiday season.

THE EASTERN COAST

Sicily's other large cities, Messina, Siracusa and Catania are on the eastern coast, and so is its most popular resort, Taormina. Remains of Roman and Greek settlements are copious, and many inland towns are built in the style of the Sicilian Baroque. Above all these places looms the fiery peak of Mount Etna, adding drama to the fascinating surroundings.

Fontana di Orione, Messina

Messina

Messina ⓭, a busy port town 200km (124 miles) east of Cefalù, is where the eastern coast starts, leading south. It is within sight of mainland Italy, with Calabria across the Strait of Messina. This is often the first place where visitors set foot on Sicily; boats ferrying cars and trains across the strait pull in and out of the harbour around the clock. The town's modern appearance and wide boulevards are the outcome of extensive rebuilding after earthquakes (the last one, in 1908, killed 85,000 residents – two-thirds of the population) and massive World War II bombings.

While most visitors hurry on to more atmospheric places, Messina rewards a short visit. The duomo in the town centre is a felicitous and determined reconstruction of the church that Roger II erected in the 12th century. The 1908 earthquake levelled the church and it was rebuilt in the 1920s, and when a 1943 firebombing laid waste to these efforts, the city built the church once again. From the heights of the campanile comes a quarter-hourly chime accompanied by a theatrical show of revolving planets, goddesses and beasts; one of them, the town's symbolic lion, roars at noon. The 16th-century **Fontana di Orione** in front of the Duomo has miraculously escaped the ravages that have befallen Messina, and so has the simple, 12th-century church of the **Annunziata dei Catalani**.

Via Garibaldi and its continuation, Via della Libertà, lead north about 2km (1.5 miles) through the centre of town to its highlight, the **Museo Regionale** (Mon–Tues and Thur–Sat 9am–1.30pm, 4–6.30pm, 3–5.30pm winter, Sun 9am–1pm; charge). This major collection has works by Antonello da Messina, Sicily's Renaissance master, including his *St Gregory* polyptych. Two of the most stunning works in the museum are by Caravaggio, the *Adoration of the Shepherds* and the *Resurrection of Lazarus*.

Taormina

Sicily's most famous resort clings to a hillside high above the sea and, is surrounded by luxurious tropical gardens that bloom year round, with Mount Etna as a backdrop. **Taormina** ❶ also retains the charm of a small, medieval hilltown. Pastel-coloured palaces and churches and a magnificent Greek

The *passeggiata* at Taormina

Theatre are tucked away on narrow, often stepped streets. These charms are not current news – D. H. Lawrence took such a shine to Taormina that he stayed three years, from 1920 to 1923. Taormina is popular with vacationers from early spring to late autumn and seethes in mid-summer. The main activity is strolling the length of its pedestrianised, narrow main street, Corso Umberto, shopping and visiting the cafés and restaurants.

Visitors arriving by taxi or bus enter the city at **Porta Messina**, the northern entrance that is a stroll from the *funivia* (cable car) that carries visitors up from the beaches below. The Corso starts here, lined with many 15th-century palazzi. One of them, the Palazzo Corvaja in the Piazza Vittorio Emanuelle, houses the tourist office, and this arrangement makes it possible to catch a glimpse of its ornamentation of black and white lava, the great hall where the Sicilian parliament met in 1410, and the elegant staircase in the courtyard.

The Teatro Greco and Giardino Pubblico

From Piazza Vittorio Emanuelle, the Via Teatro Greco leads to Taormina's beautiful **Greek Theatre** (daily 9am to one hour before sunset; charge). Though the Romans more or less rebuilt the structure, it is typically Greek in its splendid location, carved into the hillside in such a way that Mount Etna and the sea provide a permanent backdrop. As no less an observer than Goethe once exhaled into his diaries, 'Never did any audience, in any theatre, have before it such a spectacle.' The acoustics are excellent, and the theatre hosts a summer arts festival, Taormina Arte, which presents drama, cinema, ballet and music from June to October.

Via Bagnoli Croce leads downhill off the Corso to the **Giardino Pubblico**, where stands of cypress and cedar frame views of the sea. From the top of the town, a steep path climbs uphill to the ruins of the medieval castello and even higher to the little mountaintop village of Castelmola perched on a limestone peak.

But stroll along the Corso. Enjoy the shopping or refreshments. The airy Piazza IX Aprile is filled with café tables

Gole dell'Alcántara

Over the centuries the river Alcántara, fed by springs on Mount Etna, has cut a deep but enchanting canyon (www.parcoalcantara.it) into the basalt flow near Naxos (Taormina). Almost every strata of lava created by each volcanic eruption can be identified. The river bed is reached on foot down the wooded hillside or by elevator, and in summer, when the waters are low, you can walk 150m/yds safely along the bumpy river bed itself – to go any further than is permitted would lead to dangerous drops and waterfalls. The waters are cold but a visit is an exhilarating adventure and waders and wetsuits can be rented on site. Coaches depart from Taormina and Catania.

and open on one side to views of the sea and Mount Etna. Through the **Torre dell'Orologio**, a 12th-century clock tower that straddles the Corso, you come to the Piazza del Duomo, where the crenellated, fortress-like **cathedral** backs a splashing fountain. Further on you come to Porta Catania, the town's exit.

Teatro Greco, Taormina

Mount Etna

Europe's largest and most active volcano soars 3,323m (10,902ft) above the Sicilian coast. Fiery **Mount Etna** has long fascinated residents of Sicily and visitors to the island. Pindar and Pluto wrote about it, Empedocles jumped into its gaseous crater, D. H. Lawrence and legions of other noted observers have waxed poetic about it.

Sicilians keep a close eye on the volcano for good reason: molten lava flowed through Catania in 1669 and regularly plunges down the mountain towards the towns on its flanks. Eruptions occur on an almost annual basis, wreaking substantial damage on roads, houses and the tourism infrastructure on the flanks of the mountain. The volcano was particularly active in 2012, erupting dramatically several times during the year, though posing no threat to human safety. When the volcano is erupting, admirers are allowed to venture no further than Randazzo, Nicolosi and other towns and resorts in the green foothills; many can be reached on the **Circumetnea** railway, which leaves from Catania and skirts the mountain's lower flanks. Conditions permitting, **Rifugio Sapienza** is the base from which to make an ascent to the summit on foot or by the cable car (www.

Catania's cathedral

funiviaetna.com) and Jeep (see page 90).

Catania

Sicily's second largest city, 38km (24 miles) down the coast from Taormina, **Catania** ⓰ is grim and industrial in parts, but has a vibrant **historic centre** of bold Baroque buildings, boisterous food markets and cutting-edge arts and entertainment. Major restoration is ongoing, putting what was formerly a dilapidated and undervalued city on the tourist map.

Piazza del Duomo

This elegant restored square lies at the southern end of the Via Etnea. The wide boulevard, Catania's main shopping street, makes a straight run through the city towards the looming, snow-capped volcano, only 20km (12 miles) away. The square and the **Duomo** are the work of Giovanni Battista Vaccarini, who came to Catania in 1730 to rebuild the city from the rubble to which it was reduced in a 1669 lava flow and a 1693 earthquake. Vaccarini's elegant assemblage surrounds the **Fontana dell'Elefante** (Elephant Fountain), crafted like most of Catania's monuments from black lava. Water cascades around a pachyderm with an Egyptian obelisk on its back, creating a pleasing effect that Napoleon copied in several of the monuments he commissioned in Paris.

The **Duomo**'s medieval apses, built of lava, are all that survived the earthquake, and they now lie behind a Baroque façade into which Vaccarini set several columns purloined from Catania's Roman ruins. Vincenzo Bellini, the composer of *Norma* and some of the other most popular operas of the early 19th-century, is buried in the church, as is Sant' Agata, the city's patron. Agata is a venerated presence in Catania, and has even influenced the city's famous pastries, *seni di vergine* – they are shaped like her breasts, which were cut off when she was martyred. (Catania honours Bellini with *spaghetti alla Norma*, named for his famous heroine.)

Catania's raucous fish, vegetable and fruit market fills the streets to the west of the piazza; to reach the warren of stalls, step through the Porta Uzeda. This lively commerce transpires in the shadows of **Castello Ursino**, the grim fortress from which Frederick II extended a firm hand over his Sicilian kingdom. Frederick built his castle on the seashore, but molten lava from the 1669 eruption landlocked the structure. The cavernous interior houses the eclectic holdings of the **Museo Civico**, restored and ranging from archaeological finds to Baroque statuary.

Catania's fish market

Piazza Mazzini and Via dei Crociferi

From the gardens in front of the castle it is a short walk up Via Auteri to Piazza Mazzini, surrounded by arcades crafted from 32 columns salvaged from a Roman basilica. More Roman remains rise just to the west: a remarkably intact theatre from the

2nd century BC and a small Odeon used for recitations and rehearsals. Vincenzo Bellini was born in the adjoining Piazza San Francisco, and the composer's house is now the **Museo Belliniano**, filled with his original scores and other memorabilia. A nearby house and museum, just off Corso Vittorio Emanuele on Via Santa Anna, commemorates another noted Catania native, the 19th-century novelist and short story writer Giovanni Verga. Although Verga is little read outside of Italy, his stark depictions of everyday life in Sicily have earned him the reputation as one of the great Italian masters of fiction.

Piazza San Francisco is at the foot of the **Via Crociferi**, with a succession of Baroque churches, convents and noble palazzi. **San Nicolò** to the west is the largest church in Sicily and certainly the most eerie. Work was curtailed by the 1693 earthquake and the church was later abandoned, incomplete. Restoration is currently underway. The huge adjoining

Teatro Romano, Catania

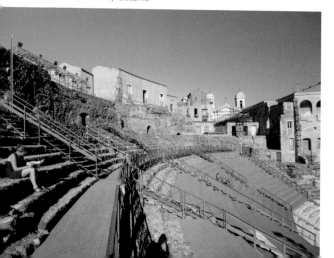

Benedictine Monastery is now part of the university; guided visits reveal internal cloisters, a hanging garden and remains of a Roman house.

Teatro Romano

At the northern end of Via Crociferi, on busy Piazza Stesicoro, looms the hulking **Teatro Romano**. Sant' Agata was thrown to the lions here in 252, before what may have been a size-able audience – the vast amphitheatre seats 16,000 spectators. Looking up Via Etnea from the front of the theatre, it is easy to comprehend the power of a local legend that claims the citizens of Catania once stopped a lava flow from the nearby mountain by waving the saint's veil in front of it. If Etna is rumbling and spewing during your visit, you may well wish you were equipped with similar protection.

Inland to Enna and Piazza Armerina

Enna ⓱, 85km (52 miles) west of Catania on autostrada A 19, is the highest city in Sicily, lying about 900m (3,000ft) above a vast plain that once supplied the Greeks and Romans with wheat. This is not, however, Sicily's most cheerful city, surrounded as it often is by mist and huddled beneath a dark fortress erected by Frederick of Swabia in the 14th century.

On a clear day the views are splendid, and the best places to enjoy them are the central square, Piazza Crispi, or better yet, the Torre Pisana, one of six towers rising above the fortress. On the plains below, wheat fields stretch for miles across the cen-tre of the island. Amid them glimmers **Lago di Pergusa**, the lake where Hades is said to have abducted Persephone, daugh-ter of Zeus and goddess of fertility, and carried her off; the wheat died in Persephone's absence, but the earth bloomed anew when Hades released her. Today the lake is surrounded by a hectic motor race track and fast food outlets.

Piazza Armerina

Most travellers pass through Piazza Armerina, on their way to the Roman villa, Villa Romana, at nearby Casale. The hill town, 35km (23 miles) south of Enna, warrants a short visit in its own right, too. The 17th-century duomo tops the town, and from the piazza the streets wind down the hillside past churches and palaces to the palm-shaded Piazza Garibaldi.

The Villa Romana at Casale

The **Villa Romana** ⑱ (open daily 8am–one hour before sunset; charge; www.romanadelcasale.org) lies 5km (3 miles) southwest of Piazza Armerina, outside the little hamlet of Casale. Co-emperor Maximian, who ruled the waning Roman Empire with Diocletian, is thought to have built this elaborate hunting lodge in the 4th century. Later, the villa was abandoned and eventually buried by landslides, and it wasn't completely unearthed until 1950. The many layers of mud that lay atop the ruins for centuries helped preserve the exquisite mosaics with which the villa is floored. Craftsmen from North Africa laid the colourful tiles, filling room after room with hunting scenes, a bestiary of exotic animals from the far corners of the empire,

Fabulous mosaics at
Villa Romana

mythical heroes and snippets of everyday life, such as a family relaxing in the baths. The villa's most famous mosaic scenario is the one depicting ten girls, clad in bikinis, competing in a gymnastics competition. Restoration at the site has been ongoing for 10 years; expect at least some rooms to be off limit (check the website for the latest information).

Ceramics at Caltagirone

Caltagirone

Citizens of the small town of **Caltagirone** ⑲, 35km (21 miles) southeast of Piazza Armerina, have been making ceramics for centuries. They show off their skill on every available surface: bridges, the 142 steps of La Scala (which climbs one of the town's three hills), the interiors of churches and the façades of houses are tiled with the town's distinctive blue-and-yellow ceramics.

Caltagirone would be attractive even without this adornment, since its old town is filled with Sicilian Baroque and Art Nouveau buildings; the church of **San Francesco d'Assisi** is an especially attractive example of the Sicilian Baroque. The **Museo della Ceramica** displays work from Caltagirone and elsewhere in Sicily, and the famous local product is for sale in workshops throughout the old town.

Siracusa (Syracuse)

What may well be Sicily's most enticing city is actually three places: the vast Greek and Roman city that played such a prominent role in the ancient world; the cultural island of Ortygia

Teatro Greco in Siracusa

(now Ortigia), where the narrow streets are lined with classical monuments and intricate Baroque churches; and a modern town of broad avenues and seaside promenades. A walk almost anywhere in **Siracusa 20**, which is 59km (37 miles) south of Catania, brings you to a remarkable structure or two.

The remains of ancient Syracuse litter every corner of the city, but many are concentrated on the mainland in the **Parco Archeologico della Neapolis** (daily 9am to two hours before sunset; charge) on the western edge of the modern city. Looking at these monuments, it is easy to appreciate the power Siracusa once wielded. Corinthians colonised Siracusa in the 8th century BC, settling on the island of Ortigia. Soon they set their eyes on the rest of Sicily and much of the Mediterranean world, defeating the Carthaginian and Etruscan fleets and eventually, in the so-called Great Expedition of 413BC, the forces Athens sent to quell the ambitious Siracusans. Under such powerful and often tyrannical rulers as Hieron I and Dionysius the Elder, the city thrived and welcomed Pindar, Aeschylus, Plato and other great minds of the Hellenistic world.

The Romans, against whom Siracusa fought in the Second Punic War, finally subdued the city in 211BC. Though Siracusa never again regained its power, natural harbours ensured the city would remain an important trading post. Early Christianity, bolstered by a visit from Saint Paul, flourished in Siracusa, and extensive catacombs beneath the city served as both tombs and churches.

The Parco Archeologico della Neapolis

Much of ancient Siracusa was built of limestone that slaves, captured in the city's numerous sea battles, dug out of quarries called the **Latomie**. Now overgrown with tropical foliage that lends a garden-like aspect to the archaeological park, the Latomie were also used as prisons. The cavern dubbed **Orecchio di Dionisio** Ⓐ, Ear of Dionysius, seems to have been especially well suited to this purpose: legend has it the tyrant made use of the unusual acoustics, which allowed him to stand at the entrance and overhear anything a prisoner or guard within might whisper. The dampness of the adjoining **Grotta dei Cordari** (closed indefinitely) provided ideal conditions for ropemakers, rendering the strands more pliant; the ropes fashioned here thousands of years ago have left deep indentations in the rocks.

Just beyond the Ear of Dionysius is the **Teatro Greco** Ⓑ, one of the largest Greek theatres in the ancient

The Ear of Dionysius, a man-made cave

world. Aeschylus wrote works to be performed on its stage. Of the original 59 rows of seats, 42 still remain and are filled during the summer months for popular performances of some of the ancient Greek dramas. The **Anfiteatro Romano ⓒ** served less refined tastes: built in the 3rd century AD, it staged circuses and gladiatorial events. Hieron II, who ruled all of Sicily from Siracusa throughout much of the 3rd century BC, commissioned his eponymous **Ara di Ierone II ⓓ**. The largest sacrificial altar in the Greek world was 200m (660ft) long and could accommodate 450 bulls at a time.

Basilica di San Giovanni and the Catacombs
Other remnants of ancient Siracusa are scattered about the city, often neglected and choked by weeds. A much-visited site is the city's oldest church, the **Basilica di San Giovanni ⓔ**, just north of Via Teocrito. Though the church has been a roofless ruin since the earthquake of 1693, it is possible to find the spot where Saint Paul delivered a sermon and the pillar to which Saint Marcian, the first bishop of Siracusa, was tied and flogged to death in 254. Steps descend to the **Catacombe di San Giovanni ⓕ**, part of a vast network of caverns that often follows the paths of subterranean Greek aqueducts. They provided a

Eureka and Archimedes

It is most unlikely Archimedes jumped from his bath crying Eureka! (Greek for 'I have found it!') on discovering the principle of specific gravity, even though physics teachers often say so. Born in Siracusa in 287BC, the great genius and theoretician worked for Hieron, the Tyrant of Siracuse, and among his inventions for his country's war were a long range catapult and a 4,000-ton ship with three decks, a gymnasium and garden. He was killed during the city's Roman occupation by a Roman soldier who failed to recognise the old man.

View over the Baroque town of Noto

art gallery, highlight of which is Antonello da Messina's *Annunciation*. Caravaggio's *Burial of St Lucy*, which used to hang here, is now in the church of Santa Lucia up the street.

Inland from Siracusa

The rocky plains and scrubby mountains that lie inland from Siracusa are littered with more ancient remains; it was here, too, that the Sicilian Baroque flowered in several small towns. On the plains 8km (5 miles) west of Siracusa, **Castello Eurialo** was the largest and most intricate fortification to survive from the ancient Greek world. Elaborate as the defences were, history would prove that they were built in vain – Siracusa eventually surrendered without a fight to the Roman legions. **Palazzolo Acrèide**, 45km (28 miles) west of Siracusa, was an early colony of ancient Siracusa, founded as **Akrai** in the 7th century BC. It's hard to get a sense of Akrai's one-time glory in the clutter of its ruins, but the lovely, semicircular **Teatro Greco** is well

Gagini, the illustrious clan of Baroque sculptors, and a fine painting of Saint Zosimus by Antonello da Messina.

Fonte Aretusa and Galleria Regionale

The western shore of Ortigia, just a few steps in front of Piazza Duomo, is the long seaside esplanade, the **Foro Italico**. This is where Siracusans come for an evening *passeggiata*, accompanied by a view of the setting sun. Lord Nelson docked here, beside the **Fonte Aretusa** ❿, to take on fresh water en route to the Battle of the Nile. He drew from a renowned source: the fountain was famous through-

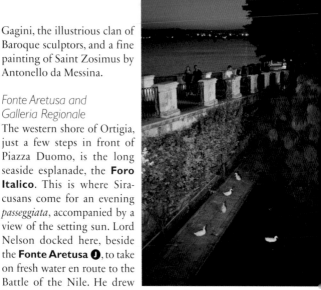

Fonte Aretusa, Ortigia

out the ancient world as the metamorphosed nymph Arethusa. Fleeing the unwanted attentions of the river god Alpheius, she called on the goddess Artemis for help. Artemis turned her into a spring, and she flowed beneath the Mediterranean and emerged here – to no avail, since Alpheius followed her and forever mingles his waters with hers. The fountain continues to gush into a pool overgrown with papyrus. The promenade running south, the Lungomare Alfeo, is flanked by seaview restaurants and bars. At its end the **Castello Maniace** ⓚ is a massive Swabian fortress which has been newly restored and opened to the public.

The Via Capodieci leads inland again to a handsome group of palaces. One of them, the 13th to 15th century **Palazzo Bellomo**, houses the **Galleria Regionale** ⓛ, the regional

the remnants of more than 2,500 years of history. After decades of neglect it has undergone regeneration and is looking lovelier than ever.

The **Tempio di Apollo**  is at the end of Ponte Nuovo. A few broken columns and marble fragments are all that remains of the structure, which dates from 565BC and is thought to be the oldest Doric temple in Sicily. This temple was dedicated to Apollo, whose name is legible on the steps of the base. The Corso Matteoti leads from the temple to Piazza Archimede, the grandiose centre of Ortigia and named for the Greek mathematician and inventor who was a 3rd-century BC resident of the city. The Piazza Duomo, just south along the Via Roma, is one of the most attractive squares in Italy, providing an appropriate setting for the cathedral and some of the island's grandest palaces.

The **Duomo** (daily 7.30am–7.30pm) is a blend of architectural styles from Siracusa's long history. It incorporates the body of a temple of Athena the Siracusans built in thanksgiving for their victory over the Carthaginians at Himera in the 6th century BC; you can see 12 columns from the temple, including one of the most splendidly decorated in the ancient world located in the north wall. The church took on Byzantine elements when it became the first Christian cathedral of Siracusa in AD640, a Norman façade that was replaced when it collapsed in the earthquake of 1693, and the Baroque elements that are much in evidence today. The interior is quite sparse, but houses a number of statues by the

Siracusa Duomo

place of refuge for Christians during times of Roman persecution, and as Christian burial was forbidden under Roman law, so the passageways also served as tombs – it is believed that more than 20,000 early Christians are buried beneath San Giovanni.

The ruins of Greek fortifications on Ortigia, Siracusa

The Museo Archeologico

Many of the finds from ancient Siracusa are displayed in the **Museo Archeologico Regionale Paolo Orsi** (Tues–Sat 9am–6pm, Sun 9am–1pm; charge) just south of San Giovanni on Via Teócrito. This is one of the most extensive archaeological collections in Europe and ranges far beyond Siracusa into the rest of the Mediterranean world. The prize of the collection, though, is from Siracusa: a headless Venus Anadiomene, modestly covering her nudity as she emerges from the water. Among the votive statuettes, burial urns and torsos, are tools and skeletons of the Stone and Bronze Age peoples who inhabited this corner of Sicily long before the Greeks arrived. The small **Museo del Papiro** next door displays ancient papyrus manuscripts and other artifacts. Ancient Siracusans are believed to have brought the plant back from their exploits in North Africa, and you may notice clumps of it in the city's gardens – the only place in Europe it grows.

Ortigia

This picturesque island, once ancient **Ortigia**, is separated from the mainland by a narrow channel, and crammed with

preserved. Among the ruins are early Christian catacombs, a necropolis, stone carvings and votive niches.

Val di Noto

The beautiful Baroque towns in southeastern Sicily, built after the terrible earthquake of 1693, were designed to be blatantly theatrical and spectacular. Eight of the towns have been designated a World Heritage Site and their historic centres are seeing a revival with buildings restored to their former glory.

Noto

When an earthquake levelled **Noto** ㉑ on 11 January 1693, architects immediately set to work rebuilding the town. The Sicilian Baroque, a flamboyantly ornamental architectural style, was in full flower, and Noto was a blank canvas on which to show it off. Today this is the finest Baroque town in Sicily, with magnificently restored churches and palaces. Corso Vittorio Emanuele and the central Piazza del Municipio are fantasies of curving staircases, elaborate balconies and porticos, and richly detailed façades. The grandest mansion is the restored **Palazzo Nicolaci di Villadorata**, with wonderfully ornate balconies and an elaborate interior with frescoed walls and ceilings.

Looking at the **Duomo** atop a dramatic staircase and the heavily colonnaded **Municipio**, it's hard to believe Noto is built of solid stone – albeit a soft local stone.

Ragusa

Ragusa ㉒, 50km (30 miles) west of Noto, is another

Best Baroque

Noto is Sicily's finest Baroque town, with all its principal buildings, palazzi and churches designed to be both theatrical and spectacular – which they are. Sicilians often dismiss it as a garden of stone, but as a Unesco Heritage Site being restored to its former glory, the town centre's monumental pomp makes it a remarkable spectacle.

Noto's cathedral

Baroque town – at least half of one, since the older Baroque section, Ragusa Ibla, is separated from the newer, more ordinary Ragusa Superiore by a deep gorge. A flight of 242 steps climbs up and down the hillsides into the quiet streets and piazzas of **Ragusa Ibla**; the church of Santa Maria delle Scale (Saint Mary of the Steps) is a welcome spot to rest midway and enjoy a stunning view over the ochre-coloured town. At the highest point of Ragusa Ibla is the Piazza Duomo and Basilica di San Giorgio, the city centrepiece. Palm trees, a curving staircase leading up to the church and a façade of columns and balconies create a masterfully Baroque scene.

Módica and Scicli

Perched on a ridge spilling down into a gorge the town of **Módica** ㉓ comprises the upper town (Módica Alta) and the lower town (Módica Bassa). This is the most prosperous town in Sicily, renowned for its chocolate, excellent shopping and gastronomy, yet it is an unpretentious sort of place and far from glitzy. The pride of Módica is the Baroque Duomo di San Giorgio perched precariously above the alleys of the historic upper town, surmounting a daunting baroque flight of 250 steps. Its rival is the opulent church of San Pietro, on the Corso, reached by another theatrical stairway.

Scicli 24, lying in a valley surrounded by rocky hills, is a gorgeous Baroque gem which is seeing a new lease of life. Palaces and churches have been skilfully restored, artisans are moving in and the town has come into its own as a film set, featuring in the *Inspector Montalbano* TV series, adapted from the detective novels by Antonio Camilleri.

THE SOUTHWESTERN COAST

Two of the ancient world's greatest cities are next to the sea on the southern coast of Sicily, and Arab colonists have left their mark as well.

Agrigento

The poet Pindar described the city the Greeks knew as Akragas as the 'fairest of mortal cities'. You probably won't disagree with the sentiment as you look upon the dramatic vestiges of the ancient city, where a row of temples follows a ridge above the sea and a valley littered with ruins set among olive trees.

Unfortunately, the modern world intrudes upon this idyllic scene rather rudely. Modern buildings, constructed illegally, encroach upon the ruins. Workaday Agrigento, which occupies a hillside above the ancient city, is undistinguished, hastily put up in the 1960s after overbuilding triggered a catastrophic mudslide. What brings visitors to Agrigento are the ruins of the ancient city spread across the so-called Valle dei Templi (Valley of the Temples).

Ruins of Castor and Pollux Temple

Valley of the Temples

Valley of the Temples

In its heyday in the 5th century BC Agrigento rivalled Athens in splendour. Founded by settlers from Rhodes and Gela in 582BC, it provided a good harbour and fertile soil and soon flourished – first under the tyrannical Phalaris, a member of a bull cult who allegedly burned his enemies alive in a bronze bull, then under Theron, who by the early 5th century BC had defeated the Carthaginians and extended the power of Akragas over much of the Mediterranean.

The city became known for its wealth and as a flourishing capital of 200,000 people who promoted the arts, philosophy and chariot racing. Empedocles, a native, developed the theory of the four elements (Earth, Air, Wind and Fire) and died when he dove into the crater of Mount Etna to investigate his premises. The philosopher had commented, 'The city's citizens enjoy life as they would die tomorrow, but they build palaces as if to live forever.' This prosperity, however, was short lived: Carthage sacked the city in 406BC, and Rome invaded in 210BC.

The arrival point of the **Valley of the Temples** ㉕ (daily Apr–June 10am–6pm, July–Sep 10am–7pm, Oct–Mar 10am–5pm; www.parcodeitempli.net; charge) is Piazzale dei Templi. The site is divided into two zones: Eastern and Western. Start with the Eastern zone, which has the main temples. The first and the oldest is the **Tempio di Ercole (Hercules) Ⓐ**, dating from the 6th century BC and now a romantic jumble of ruins from which nine of its original columns still emerge. A statue of Hercules and a fresco depicting the young god grappling with serpents once graced the temple, but these have long since vanished.

Follow Via Sacra to the superbly sited **Tempio della Concordia Ⓑ**. Built around 450BC, this is the best preserved temple at Agrigento (largely because it was converted to a Christian church in the 6th century), and one of the finest Doric temples of the ancient world. The stucco that once covered the temple has long since worn away, exposing warm, golden stone. At the end of Via Sacra stands the **Tempio di Giunone (Juno) Ⓒ**, which was built by the Greeks in 460BC, and restored by the Romans after the handsome structure was destroyed by the Carthaginians; the stones are still scorched from the fires the invaders set. Earthquakes have also taken their toll, though a sacrificial altar and 25 of the 34 original columns have been set back in place.

In the Western Zone the stony remains of the **Tempio di Giove Olimpico (Jove) Ⓓ** are copious enough to suggest that this was indeed the largest Doric temple ever built. Enormous *telamones* (columns fashioned in the shape of male figures) once supported the massive structure, and a reproduction of one of them, the so-called Gigante, lies on the ground among the ancient debris. West of the temple is a puzzling quarter dotted with pagan shrines. The Giardino della Kolymbetra (extra charge) is a large and fertile garden of citrus and other trees which has been restored and creates a delightful diversion from the temples.

The Museo Archeologico and the Roman City
The **Museo Archeologico Regionale Ⓔ** (Tues–Sun 9am–7pm, Mon 9am–1pm; charge) holds a wealth of artefacts

Entrance gate into Sciacca

excavated from the Valley of the Temples. Delicate vases, terracotta figurines, and an alabaster sarcophagus designed for a young boy and etched with scenes from his childhood provide an evocative glimpse into life in the ancient city. One room is dedicated to the Tempio di Giove Olimpico, with reconstructions of the temple and a reassembled *telamon*. Next to the museum spread the remains of the settlement that the Romans established when they took Agrigento permanently in 210BC. Many of the houses they constructed on the Greek streets still stand, and their mosaic flooring is remarkably intact.

Modern Agrigento

The modern city also bears some traces of Agrigento's ancient inhabitants: **Santa Maria dei Greci** **F**, a small basilica rising above the stepped streets of the medieval quarter, is built of antique materials on the site of a temple to Athena; several columns are imbedded in the walls of the church. **Santo Spirito** **G** is the church of a late 13th-century Cistercian convent whose nuns specialise in making almond and pistachio pastries (ring the doorbell marked 'monastero' next to the church to buy some). The church is rather dilapidated but inside has fine Baroque stuccowork attributed to Giacomo Serpotta.

Luigi Pirandello, Agrigento's acclaimed 20th-century novelist and dramatist, was born in the seaside suburb of **Caos**. His birthplace, the **Casa Natale di Luigi Pirandello**, is now a museum, and his ashes are buried beneath a lone pine tree in the garden.

Sciacca

This unspoiled seaside town of **Sciacca** ㉖, 65km (41 miles) northwest of Agrigento, is still engaged in the pursuits that have occupied its citizens for millennia: fishing in the waters between Sicily and Africa and ministering to patrons of its thermal spa. Residents of ancient Selunis, just down the coast, came here to soak in the warm, mineral-rich waters that emerge from deep beneath nearby Monte San Calogero, and the thermal station still provides a full regimen of treatments. The town that climbs the hillside above the busy fishing port is flat-roofed and whitewashed, a legacy of many years of Arab habitation. Among the later structures rising above the warren of little stepped streets are the 17th-century Duomo and the simpler, 12th-century church of **San Nicolò La Latina**.

Caltabellotta ㉗, a small mountain village that clings to three rocky promontories high in the mountains above Sciacca, played an important role in Sicilian history. In its now-ruined castle, Charles of Valois and Frederick of Aragon signed the treaty that ended the 13th-century revolt against French rule known as the War of the Vespers.

Taking it easy

Temple at Selinunte

Selinunte

The city the ancient Greeks knew as Selunis (for the wild celery that still grows in abandon around the ruins) had little time to play an important role in the affairs of classical Sicily. Citizens were still building their city when Hannibal attacked in 409BC; Selunis never recovered, and earthquakes have since levelled the remains.

Even so, **Selinunte** ㉘ (9am to one hour before sunset; charge), 45km (27 miles) west of Sciacca, is one of the most evocative ancient sites in the Mediterranean, with ruined temples and monuments that now stand in lonely fields next to the sea. Three of the temples have been partially restored. They are designated by letter rather than name; to whom they were dedicated remains uncertain. **Temple E** is closest to the sea, and its massive columns have been set upright. The temple was possibly dedicated to Juno, wife of Zeus. **Temple G** was one of the largest Doric structures in Greek Sicily, though it was never completed; unfinished column blocks lie among its rubble. **Temple C**, which dates around mid-6th-century BC, stands at the highest point of the acropolis on the knoll of the hill and is the largest temple of all. The giant columns are nearly 2 m (6.5ft) in diameter, except for those on the temple corners which are even thicker. It has provided the archaeological museum in Palermo with some of its greatest treasures – the metopes, or decorative friezes, that were once set atop its columns. A lengthy visit to the sprawling site can be followed by a swim along the sandy coast. The new settlement, **Marinella di Selinunte**, is a fishing port and resort, lined with lively restaurants.

THE WEST COAST

Western Sicily was settled by Phoenicians, Greeks, Romans, Arabs, and the great European powers of the Middle Ages, and their presence is still much in evidence.

Mazara del Vallo

Mazara del Vallo  may be of Phoenician origin but Arab influences predominate, from the Tunisian trawlermen to the Arab music and shisha hubble-bubble pipes. However the Kasbah with its maze of backstreets has been newly gentrified with freshly painted houses and ceramic plaques and murals. The town has a long and pleasant tree-shaded seafront, with marina and beach, and a centre of fine churches. Within a deconsecrated church the **Museo del Satiro** (Satyr Museum, daily 9am–6.30am; charge) houses the 4th century BC bronze satyr, known as the Dancing Satyr. This was hauled up from the seabed by local fishermen and underwent a restoration in Rome. The statue is 6.5ft high and although both arms and a leg are missing you can see that the satyr is performing a wild ecstatic dance, his head thrown back and his hair flowing.

Garibaldi gate,
Marsala

Marsala

The sleepy city of **Marsala** ㉚, 70km (43 miles) north and west of Selinunte, has a long and raucous past. The Phoenicians settled here in the 8th century BC, abandoned the city when they made the island of **Mozia** their stronghold, and came back when the Siracusans routed them in 397BC. After a ten-year siege, the Romans took the city in 241BC. Lilybaeum, as the city was then called, become the seat of the Roman governor of Sicily; by the time Caesar arrived on his way to Africa in 47BC, Cicero had dubbed Lilybaeum a *civitas splendidissima*.

The port also proved to be a convenient gateway for the Arabs who overran Sicily in the 9th century; they called it 'the harbour of Allah', or *Marsa al Allah*. On 11 May 1860, the port of Marsala welcomed Garibaldi and the Thousand, the red-shirted freedom fighters who freed Sicily from Bourbon rule to unite Italy as a republic. Marsala bears its past glories with modesty. Of the ancient city, little remains but fragments of the Roman walls, some baths and a 3rd-century villa that's decorated with mosaics of hunting scenes and the four seasons. These are concentrated in the

Marsala Wine

In 1773 English merchant John Woodhouse shipped 60 barrels of golden Marsala wine to England, adding a dose of alcohol to ensure it would survive the journey. The wine was an instant success and was soon stocked by the British navy, but Marsala later lost its reputation and was more or less relegated to cooking purposes. Recent years have seen a renaissance, with producers – no longer English – producing dry, smooth dessert wines, aged in oak barrels and known as Vergine or Riserva. The market leader is Florio (Via Vincenzo Florio 1, tel: 0923 78111), where you can taste various types of Marsala.

archaeological zone on the **Capo Boeo** promontory at the western edge of the city, which also happens to be the westernmost point in Sicily.

The nearby **Museo Archeologico** (Tues–Sun 9am–7pm, Mon 9.30am–1pm; charge) displays more Roman finds, including some colourful wall paintings and Phoenician ceramics. Most interesting, though, is a **Phoenician warship** that the Romans probably sank in the

Marsala Cathedral

First Punic War. Discovered in 1971 on the seabed just north of Marsala, the boat is one of the few warships to survive from antiquity and has provided archaeologists with a wealth of information about the arts of ancient warfare.

The Old Town

The sweet, pleasant scent that pervades the city is that of an elixir that brought Marsala fame and fortune in the 18th century – Marsala wine (see box). British warships sent to protect England's interests in the Marsala business proved to be convenient for Garibaldi, who assumed they would also protect him when he made his landing here in 1860.

Garibaldi's presence in Marsala is commemorated by the Porta Garibaldi and the Via Garibaldi, which leads north from the port to the **Piazza della Repubblica**, the centre of town. The **Palazzo Comunale** and the **Duomo** face the square. Both have Baroque, 18th-century façades; sculptures by Antonello Gagini decorate the church.

Young Man in a Tunic,
5th-century BC statue
at the Museo Whitaker

Mozia

The Phoenicians colonised the tiny island of San Pantelo in the 8th century BC and built **Mozia** ㉛, one of their three cities on Sicily, set within a ring of ramparts and towers. They remained until Dionysius, the power-hungry Siracusan, routed them in 397BC.

The Phoenicians went back and forth across the lagoon on a raised road, which now lay submerged beneath the shallow waters. Today's visitors reach the island by the ferry that departs from a landing stage opposite the island. The mainland near San Pantelo is marshy and parceled into salt pans, and windmills that were once used to refine the salt rise above the flat landscape. One of the mills near the landing, the **Mulino Salina Infersa**, houses a small museum devoted to salt extraction.

Joseph Whitaker, from a prosperous family of Marsala wine exporters, bought the island and began to excavate the ruins in 1913. His finds lay scattered across the tiny, almost deserted island, and include the remains of the city walls, Punic dry dock (Cothon), a sacrificial site (Tophet), and a house with a floor of pebble mosaics. The **Museo Whitaker** (daily 9.30am–1.30pm, 2–6.30pm; charge) displays Punic and Greek finds from the island including the famous *Giovane in Tunica*, Young Man in a Tunic, an exquisite, 5th-century BC marble statue of a sinuous young man who may have been a charioteer.

Trápani

This city, 32km (19 miles) north of Marsala, has been a lively port town since Phoenician times and was once the centre of trade in coral, tuna and salt with the Levant, Carthage and Venice. Until recently it was seen as a workaday city in which to kill time before the next ferry to the islands. But **Trápani** ❷ now has an elegant **historic centre** with restored churches and palaces, and a new seafront promenade. The old city is squeezed onto a narrow promontory that juts far into the sea, and the outskirts trail off into salt marshes where windmills catch Mediterranean breezes.

The sprawling modern outskirts are hardly welcoming but once in the old town it's well worth taking the time to stroll down the Corso Vittorio Emanuele to the **Torre di Ligny**, a recently restored squat Spanish fortress, built in 1671, at the end of the promontory. The street is lined with Baroque palaces and churches, and the sea poetically frames the end of the narrow side streets.

Trápani's airport is now an arrival point for low cost carriers, and from its port ferries sail to the Egadi Islands (see page 82) and Pantelleria (see page 83) as well as to Genova and Livorno, further away on mainland Italy.

Erice

Just 10km (6 miles) northeast of Trápani, **Erice** ❸ is a world apart from that city or any place else in the modern world. Isolated on the heights of Monte Erice, the town has

Cable car

Linking Trápani and Erice, the Funierice cable car (closed Mon and mid-March to second week of Jan; www.funiviaerice.it) takes just 12 minutes and affords wonderful views of saltpans, mountains, sea and islands.

always enjoyed a lofty status. The ancient Elymians called the city Eryx and built a temple dedicated to Aphrodite (the Roman Venus), goddess of fertility. Aside from gathering fame throughout the Mediterranean world for its rich decoration, the temple served as a beacon for sailors navigating the trade routes to and from Africa. The Romans restored the temple several times; the Arabs considered the town holy enough to dub it *Gebel-Hamed*, Mohammed's Mountain; and the Norman Count Roger had visions of St Julian while besieging Erice and renamed it Monte San Giuliano. Even Mussolini saw the sanctity of the town and revived its ancient name.

The Normans built their **Castello di Venere** on the site of the ancient temple, taking advantage of the commanding position at the top of the town. Erice's public gardens now surround the castle, and from them rises the 15th-century **Torretta Pepoli**. Both castle and tower are ivy-covered, and the views from the garden terraces, over the plains and sea far below, are expansive – in fact, some keen-eyed observers claim to have seen all the way to Cap Bon in Tunisia.

The rest of the town is mostly medieval and clings precipitously to the shoulder of the summit. Battlements atop the tower of the stone **Chiesa Madre** are evidence of the double duty it did for the armies of Frederick III of Aragon, who used it as a lookout post; the interior of the church is surprisingly light and airy. Its campanile dates from 1315. At the heart of the city is its only square, Piazza Umberto I. Erice is a pleasant place to stop for a few days, and is within easy reach of most of the sights on the western and southern coasts.

Segesta

The Elymians, who lavished such attention on the temple in Erice (see page 79), settled **Segesta** 🟤 (daily 9am to one hour before sunset; charge) in the 12th century BC. By the 5th century BC, when Segesta's temple was built, the city had been heavily influenced by the Greeks who had colonised the island. It was busy warring with Selinunte, its neighbour on the southern coast.

The temple and a well-preserved theatre 4km away (with shuttle bus service) are the only sizeable remains of the ancient city, which is still being excavated. Their isolation, in green hills about 30km (18 miles) east of Trápani, lend the site a singular beauty. Both are among the finest monuments of antiquity, and both are set on hills looking over the rolling countryside and the sea.

Capo San Vito

This mountainous cape at the northwestern tip of Sicily, 40km (25 miles) north of Trápani, has the finest beaches on the island around the resort of **San Vito lo Capo** ⑮ and rugged headlands that are ideal for hiking. In the **Riserva Naturale**

Greek theatre at Segesta

Sunset over the Egadi Islands

dello Zingaro ❸❻, a beautiful nature preserve just to the southeast, paths follow 6km (4 miles) of forested coastline, home to falcons and buzzards and etched with lovely coves.

The Egadi Islands (Isole Egadi)

Trápani is the jumping-off point for the three **Egadi Islands** ❸❼ in this sparsely populated archipelago. The nearest and largest island, Favignana, is only 25 minutes away by hydrofoil.

The crystalline waters are a paradise for swimmers and scuba divers and all of the islands offer good walks across unspoiled landscapes. **Favignana** is the most populated, though only 4,400 people live on the island and the number has decreased with the decline of the late-spring *La Mattanza*, the great tuna massacre which would see fishermen net and harpoon hundreds of tuna at a time. However the recent restoration of the Tonnara di Favignana, a former tuna cannery and now a tuna heritage museum, has given the island a new focus.

On barren **Levanzo**, prehistoric inhabitants of the cave now known as the **Grotta del Genovese** left behind Neolithic paintings and Paleolithic carved drawings, mostly of animals. You can reach the caves by boat from the port in Levanzo town, or walk to them along the island's only road and a dirt path; both routes provide views of the **Faraglione**, a rocky spire erupting from the sea.

Marettimo is the most isolated of the islands, and unlike Favignana and Levanzo, is mountainous and verdant. Any resemblance this lovely landscape bears to those described in ancient myth may not be coincidental: it's been suggested that Marettimo is Ithaca, the home to which Odysseus yearned to return.

Pantelleria

This windswept island of **Pantelleria** ❸❽ is closer to North Africa than it is to the rest of Sicily, 110km (66 miles) from Trápani and 70km (42 miles) from Tunisia. Pantelleria can be reached by plane or boat from Trápani and by plane from Palermo. The island also provides the opportunity to experience an unusual climatic phenomenon, a constant breeze that gives Pantelleria its name, from the Arabic *bint-al-rian*.

A good network of buses provides transport to most spots of interest, including the island's few manmade attractions. These include remnants of prehistoric settlers of which the most fascinating is **Sesi**, a collection of funeral mounds on the southwest coast in which black volcanic rock is piled into high mounds. More in evidence are the island's distinctive traditional white-washed *dammusi* houses, first introduced by Arab colonists.

Similarly exotic is the island's black soil, the legacy of its volcanic peak. The volcanic presence also accounts for the hot springs that bubble up around the island. Some of the most appealing are at **Scauri**, not far from Sesi, where you can soak in warm natural pools and then jump into the sea.

WHAT TO DO

Aside from the extensive historical sites and sights, Sicily provides a host of other diversions. Many of these activities allow you to enjoy the island's beautiful landscapes of seacoasts and mountains.

SHOPPING

Although Sicily now has its first designer mall (see under Fashion), shopping on the island is not so much about Gucci or Armani as atmospheric street markets, ceramic workshops, black-lava souvenirs and gastronomy. The best shopping is in Palermo, Catania and Taormina. In Palermo, most of the better shops are concentrated around Piazza Verdi and Via della Libertà. In Taormina, the Corso Umberto is lined with fine but small shops. Catania's Via Etnea, especially between Piazza Stesicoro and Piazza del Duomo, is the main shopping precinct. There are food and drink temptations wherever you go: chocolate from Módica, pastries from Noto, pistachios from Bronte and dessert wines (Moscato and Malvasia) from the Aeolian islands.

Antiques. Some of the most distinctive items to show up in antiques shops are pieces of the painted carts *(carretti siciliani)* that were once the mainstay of transport in the countryside. You can occasionally find plaques of wood from the carts covered in bright designs in the antiques shops of Palermo, Erice and Taormina. Another place to look for them is among the stalls of the daily flea market behind the cathedral in Palermo.

Ceramics. The town of Caltagirone, southwest of Catania, has been producing ceramics for centuries – even the 142

Ballarò market, Palermo

Santa Stéfano di Camastra ceramics

steps of its monumental staircase are covered in colourful tiles of local manufacture. Workshops around the town continue to make and sell tiles and other ceramics goods. Santo Stefano di Camastra, on the northern coast, also makes excellent ceramics.

Crafts. Erice is known for its hand-loomed cotton rugs, and they are available in several shops in town. In Taormina, several shops sell embroidered linens. Many villagers on the island still weave baskets, and sell them at local markets.

Fashion. Sicilia Outlet Village (www.siciliaoutletvillage.it) in Agira, just east of Enna, is Sicily's first luxury designer shopping mall where fashions are discounted by 30–70 percent. For fashion elsewhere head to the boutiques of Taormina, Palermo or Catania where you can find designer clothes from Valentino, Coverik, Gucci and Armani.

Papyrus. The ancients brought this African plant to Siracusa, and the city is now the only place in Europe where it grows.

The Museo del Papiro there demonstrates how the reeds are made into paper and a few craftspeople sell sheets of papyrus and other small objects made from it.

Souvenirs. Aside from the glowing replicas of Mount Etna and all manner of items made from black lava, look for the delightful replicas of the puppets that are the stars of Sicily's popular puppet theatres. The Museo Internazionale delle Marionette in Palermo (see page 37) can direct you to craftspeople who make the most authentic replicas of the puppets.

Weekly Markets

Sicilian street markets provide most of the staples of life, and vendors sell clothing, household items, hardware, appliances and an enormous variety of food, including fresh fruit, vegetables, seafood, meat and cheese. In most you'll also come upon stalls selling fast food, such as fried calamari, and in the large, daily markets in bigger cities there are usually several excellent restaurants. Any town of any size in Sicily has a market at least one day a week, usually in the morning.

In Palermo, the two largest markets in the centre of the city are the Ballarò, around Piazza Carmine in the Albergheria quarter (see page 29); and the Vucciria, in a warren of streets near the intersection of Via Roma and Corso Vittorio Emanuele. Both are held daily except Sunday. There is also a daily flea market in the streets behind the cathedral. In Catania, the market fills the streets between Piazza Duomo and Castello Ursino.

Puppet workshop in Siracusa

SPORTS AND OUTDOOR ACTIVITIES

Sicily has increasing appeal for active visitors. Coasts, islands and mountains lend themselves to year-round sporting activities. You can hike in hills and mountains, explore the underwater sea world, quad bike on Etna, wade through gorges and explore offshore islands.

Cycling. Urban leisure cycling has yet to take off on mainland Sicily, but demand has risen from visitors in recent years. Typical bike tours, offered by agencies, include Etna, the Val di Noto, the Marsala coast or the offshore islands, where cycling is particularly popular and reflects the slower pace of life. Most of the islands have mountain bikes to rent at the port.

Hiking. Sicily's rugged terrain is well suited to hiking, though there are relatively few established trail networks. An exception is the Madonie mountains, where marked trails ascend the peak of Pizzo Carbonara (1,979m/6,495ft) and crisscross the wooded terrain beneath them; the tourist office in Cefalù can provide information. The Riserva Naturale dello Zingaro (www.riservazingaro.it) protects the coast just east of Capo San Vito, and its trails follow the sea – from them you can scramble down to secluded coves – and cut through forest-covered mountainsides. The volcanic landscapes of Etna exert an obvious pull for hikers but it is advisable to take a guide. The Aeolian and Egadi islands offer excellent opportunities for hiking, from climbing the craters of Vulcano and Strómboli to off-the-beaten

Hikers on Vulcano in the Aeolian Islands

track exploration of remote Filicudi or Maréttimo.

Scuba diving and snorkeling. The waters off Ustica, a tiny island 60km (36 miles) north of Palermo, provide the best locale for both activities. A stretch of the coastline is designated as a natural marine reserve, and equipment rentals and dive schools are plentiful. The tourist office in Palermo (see page 131) provides information on Ustica's underwater activities.

Skiing. While Sicily will never be an internationally renowned ski resort, its higher peaks have lifts and other facilities. The ski resorts on Etna are Linguaglossa on

The beach at Cefalù

the northern side and Nicolosi on the southern side. In the Madonie mountains, the main ski resort is the alpine village of Piano Battaglia; the tourist information in Cefalù can provide information (see page 131).

Swimming. The beaches at Sicily's famous seaside resorts of Cefalù and Taormina are adequate but crowded, and the same can be said of Mondello, the seaside getaway for Palermo. You'll find more isolation on the beaches on Capo San Vito and, especially, in the adjoining Zingaro nature reserve, where you may be able to find a secluded cove of your own. Some of the most enjoyable swimming is from the beaches on the islands off Sicily – especially Maréttimo in the Egadi Islands and the less-crowded of the Aeolians.

Volcano Viewing. Sicily has two of the few active volcanoes in Europe, Mount Etna on the island's eastern coast and Strómboli in the Aeolian Islands. Conditions permitting, you can begin an ascent to the crater area on Etna from Rifugio Sapienza on foot or by cable car to the Rifugio Montagnola, from where you can continue on foot or in a Jeep. Tour agencies offer full day excursions to Mount Etna from Taormina; the tourist office there can provide information (see page 131).

The volcano on Strómboli puts on an around-the-clock performance: every 20 minutes or so, the crater hurls glowing multi-coloured chunks of lava into the sky, down a cliff (called the Sciara del Fuoco) and into the sea, where they hiss and steam. You can witness this spectacle from a viewpoint that is a safe distance from the activity and reached by a well-marked path; a guided ascent takes you closer to the action and is most rewarding at night. You can also view the spectacle from boats that leave from the island's tiny port, where several private agencies offer tours and provide information on how to view the volcano by land or sea.

MUSIC AND THE PERFORMING ARTS

Some of the most memorable performances in Sicily are the seasonal events held in the island's Greek theatres. Between May and June different dramatic cycles are performed in amphitheatres from Siracusa and Segesta to Selinunte, Agrigento and Morgantina. In **Taormina**, the Greco-Roman theatre draws visitors from around the world for its annual summer arts festival (www.indofondazione.org), which includes classical drama as well as opera, dance and music.

Palermo offers a great season of opera, ballet and concerts at the Teatro Massimo (www.teatromassimo.it) in Piazza Verdi, and other concerts are performed in churches around the city. Classical and jazz concerts are held in the cloisters and roofless

Palermo's Teatro Massimo

church of Lo Spasimo, an evocative entertainment complex set in a former 16th century monastery in the La Kalsa quarter.

Teatro Massimo Bellini in **Catania** (www.teatromassimo-bellini.it), named after the composer Vincenzo Bellini, is a world-famous venue for operas and concerts from October through May, and throughout the summer the city's Baroque churches and an outdoor stage in Piazza Bellini are the settings for concerts of classical and popular music. Catania is cooler for a young crowd than Palermo, with its late-night bars, live music venues, jazz and blues. As an energetic university city it offers events ranging from pop-rock spectaculars to open-air summer festivals. Zò (www.zoculture.it) is the futuristic new culture and arts centre, housed in an ex-sulphur refinery.

Erice's churches and other venues open their doors for performances of medieval and Renaissance music throughout the summer; **Noto** hosts concerts from January to June while its Baroque churches and convents are the venues for the

International Music Festival in July and August; and the glittering, mosaic-filled cathedral in **Monreale** is the setting for a festival of ecclesiastic music during the first week of November.

Puppet Theatre

This lively entertainment, with its elaborate costumes, nonstop action and touches of humour, has been delighting Sicilian children and adults for centuries. Even audiences who don't speak Italian and aren't familiar with the tales, which are usually based on exploits of knights in the court of Charlemagne, find this spectacle engrossing. In Palermo, the Museo Internazionale delle Marionette regularly stages performances. Palermo's Teatro di Via Bara (www.figlidartecuticchio.com) presents reinterpreted versions of traditional puppet theatre. Plays featuring puppets can also be seen in Acireale, Catania and Siracusa.

Puppet theatre

A puppet show is usually part of the festivities at fairs and other public celebrations in Sicily. Travelling troops tour the island in the summer months, often making stops in the resorts. Local tourist offices can let you know where and when you can find performances.

CHILDREN'S SICILY

Portraits in Palermo

Sicilians shower attention on their children, and will probably do the same with yours. Welcome as children are in museums, restaurants and just about any other place in Sicily, you may want to seek out some activities that will provide a break from trudging through ruins and archaeological museums. Some suggestions:

Cefalù and **Taormina** are pleasant to visit with children, because the low-key, car-free old towns provide plenty of diversions (especially the Greek theatre and views of Mount Etna in Taormina), and both beaches and countryside are nearby. Piazza IX Aprile in Taormina is a great place to people-watch and is full of outdoor entertainers and artists painting the wonderful views. **Erice**, ideally reached by the panoramic cable car from Trápani, is also a good place for young travellers to unwind, and they can wander the medieval streets, explore the ruined castle and enjoy the stunning views.

In **Palermo** a walk through the Vucciria market will provide plenty of diversions, as will a stroll along the rebuilt Foro

Traditional painted cart

Italico, the new seafront. The Arab and Norman sights, with their whiff of exoticism, will be popular – especially the cathedral in Monreale, with its mosaics and cloisters, and the church of San Giovanni degli Eremiti, with its gardens.

Of the classical sights, **Selinunte** is probably the most child-friendly, because of the lack of crowds and its nearby beaches and adjoining fishing port. With their volcanic peaks, black sand beaches and blue waters, the **Aeolian Islands** might appear like a magic kingdom to youngsters (after all, this archipelago has inspired many a myth) and the trip from island to island on ferry can be fun. **Stromboli**, with its ever-active volcano, is always fascinating to view and sure to please. Of course, an ascent up **Mount Etna** is mandatory; a trip around its lower flanks on the Circumetnea railway may be the best approach if the young ones aren't up to arduous treks across the lava. The Roman mosaics at **Casale** will enchant even a sight-weary child.

Parents with very young children in tow may want to avoid the treasuries of churches, which are often filled with withered extremities and other ghoulish relics. A visit to **Palermo**'s Catacombe del Convento dei Cappuccini, where thousands of preserved corpses are draped about the premises, may or may not be appropriate, depending on a child's age and sensitivities. The catacombs in **Siracusa**, meanwhile, are corpse-less but spooky and atmospheric nonetheless.

Calendar of Events

Sicilians celebrate festivals year round. The following are just a few of the many events held throughout the island.

6 January In Piana degli Albanesi outside of Palermo, costumed citizens join a procession to celebrate Epiphany.

February–March Many towns celebrate Carnevale, most notably Sciacca, Cefalù, Taormina, and Acireale, north of Catania.

Holy Week Erice, Noto, Enna, Trápani, Marsala, and many other towns note this solemn religious period with special observations; however, in San Fratello, in the hills above Cefalù, citizens celebrate the Festa dei Giudei (Feast of the Jews) by donning costumes and parading through the streets on Maundy Thursday and Good Friday.

27–29 June Sciacca hosts a big fish fry.

10–15 July All of Palermo takes to the streets for a boisterous festival in honour of Santa Rosalia, the city's patron.

Late-July International festival of cinema, dance and music in Taormina's Greek theatre.

First week of August Siracusa hosts its *palio*, in which boats manned by crews from the town's five quarters race around Ortigia.

15 August (Ferragosta) The resort of Capo d'Orlando, east of Cefalù, celebrates the Feast of the Assumption with a procession of boats. Piazza Armerina's Palio dei Normanni is a medieval pageant.

24 August The island of Lípari celebrates the feast of San Bartolomeo with fireworks and a procession around a statue of the saint.

8 September The sanctuary of the Black Madonna in Tindari is a pilgrimage destination.

September Couscous festival in San Vito Lo Capo, when chefs compete to make the best couscous. Music and dancing too.

December Opera season begins in Palermo. Taormina celebrates the Christmas season with concerts and puppet shows and kicks off the New Year with a spectacular fireworks display.

13 December Siracusans carry a silver statue of their patron, Santa Lucia, through the streets to commemorate her feast.

EATING OUT

Sicilian cuisine will probably be among the more pleasurable discoveries you make on the island. In general, it is lighter, spicier and healthier than the cuisines of many other parts of Italy. Cooks rely heavily on the three staples that are plentiful on the island: vegetables that grow year-round, fish, especially *tonno* (tuna) and *pesce spada* (swordfish), and local olive oil. Capers, raisins, wild fennel and ingredients that are often the legacy of the island's Arab heritage lend a faintly exotic flavour to many dishes, and even couscous creeps onto menus in the south and west of Sicily.

Like fish, meat, especially steak or veal, is a presence on menus, but not nearly as important a part of the local cuisine as it is to cooking elsewhere in Italy. As the island is famed for its fruit and vegetables, they play an essential role in every kitchen and vegetarians will invariably find dishes on a menu to their liking. Pasta sauces too are often made with vegetables and perhaps the island's best-known culinary contribution is *Spaghetti alla Norma*, named for the heroine of the opera by native son Vincenzo Bellini and made with eggplant (aubergines), tomatoes and fresh ricotta. Sicilian desserts are very sweet, typically made with pastry and ricotta, or marzipan in the shape of fruits.

Where to Eat

Restaurants are usually referred to as *trattoria* or *ristorante*, and though the terms have come to denote establishments of similar character, in principal at least they are quite different. A trattoria is casual, serving home-style fare in an informal setting; a ristorante implies smarter décor, more polished service and more elaborate, more expensive cuisine. Some of the more formal establishments in Palermo and Taormina affect

Eating out in Liparí

the ambiance of the latter, but most Sicilian eateries are of the family-run trattoria variety.

Bars in Sicily and elsewhere in Italy are not just places to drink alcoholic beverages. They sell wine and spirits, as well as soft drinks, mineral water and coffee. They also serve light fare: pastries *(cornetti* or *brioche)* both of which are croissants filled with jam, custard, or chocolate in the morning, little sandwiches *(tramezzino)* and filled flat rolls *(panini)* or other light dishes throughout the day. All these foods are usually displayed on the counter, you need only point to what you want.

Many Sicilians will stop by their local bar several times a day for a quick coffee and chat, and you should find one you like and do the same – there's almost no better place in which to observe the engaging drama of day-to-day Sicilian life.

Yet another type of eating establishment is the *tavola calda* or *rosticceria,* both of which are cafeteria-style eateries where several selections of hot dishes are prepared daily and served from a counter. You generally pay in advance and take the receipt to someone behind the counter, who prepares a plate for you. Pizzerias appear in every Sicilian town, and often prepare their pizzas in traditional wood-burning ovens.

Sicily has a long tradition of street food, especially in Palermo and Catania. Food markets are the best sources. Look out for chickpea fritters (*pannelle*), potato croquettes with anchovy and caciocavallo cheese (*crocche di patate*), fried rice balls with chopped meat and peas (*arancini*) and beef spleen or tripe roll (*pani cu'la meusa*).

A *caffè* and its kindred *pasticcerie* usually serve pastries and other sweets (often ice cream, or *gelato*) and sometimes light meals, accompanied by coffee, tea, or a glass of wine. An establishment or two like this grace the main piazzas of most towns in Sicily.

Family in front of a display of marzipan fruit *(frutti alla Martorana)*

One more essential stop when travelling in Sicily is a *gelateria*, a shop that sells only *gelato* (ice cream) and *sorbetto*, which is usually made with fresh fruit. Some distinctive Sicilian flavours are jasmine *(gelsomino)*, mulberry *(gelsi)* and pistachio *(pistacchio)*. When choosing a gelateria, look for queues of locals (who usually know where to find the best *gelato* in town) and for a sign that says *produzione propria*, which means 'made on the premises'. No trip to Mondello, the seaside retreat near Palermo, is complete without a stop at Renato, a famous *gelateria* in the centre of town on Piazza Mondello.

When to Eat

In Sicily, lunch is from 12.30pm to 3pm, and dinner from 7.30 or 8pm to 10.30pm. A restaurant will occasionally keep later hours, but rarely past 11pm or so. Most establishments close one day a week and occasionally for lunch or dinner immediately preceding or following the closing – so a restaurant that is closed on Monday may also close for Sunday dinner or Tuesday lunch. In the resorts, however, many restaurants keep longer hours in summer, and some close from November to March. Cafés are usually open from 8am to 11pm; bars tend to keep longer hours, especially in busy resort towns, from 7am or so until as late as 2am.

Most restaurants in Sicily include a service charge in the bill (usually 10-15 percent of the total), and many add a small *coperto* (cover charge) as well.

What to Eat

Menus are divided into *antipasti* (appetisers), *primi* (first courses), *secondi* (second courses), *contorni* (side dishes) and *dolci* (desserts). While Italian diners may include all of these elements in a meal, ordering a pasta dish or a *secondo* and a *contorno* is acceptable, especially at lunch. A meal in Sicily is to be enjoyed and lingered over, and the experience is all the better if you dine outdoors, an experience that is commonplace because of the island's balmy climate.

Following are some of the items you are likely to find on many Sicilian menus.

Antipasto means 'before the meal', and antipasti (plural) are usually cold starters served in small portions.

There is often an array of vegetables, from peppers in oil (*peperonata*) to stuffed tomatoes (*pomodori ripieni*) or *prosciutto con melone* (parma ham and melon). Aubergines are a staple, whether grilled, fried, rolled and stuffed (*involtini di melanzane*), or baked in a parmesan and tomato sauce (*melanzane alla parmigiana*).

Pizza in Liparí

A classic dish is *caponata*, fried peppers, aubergines, tomatoes, courgettes, celery and olives. The sea provides inspiration for the classic *insalata di mare*, a seafood salad tossed in a dressing of oil, lemon and herbs and *pesce spade affumicato*, smoked swordfish.

Il Primo is the first course, and in Sicily that generally means pasta, which is often made with fresh seafood.

Under the Arabs, Sicily was the first place to produce dried pasta on a commercial scale. Typical Sicilian *primi* are: *Maccu*, a creamy soup made from chickpeas, *pasta all'arrabbiata*, with a spicy sauce of tomatoes and anchovies, *pasta con broccoli*, with fresh broccoli and often anchovies, *pasta con la mollica*, with breadcrumbs, capers, olives and anchovies or *con seppia*, with cuttlefish served in its own ink. Two of the favourite *primi* are *pasta con le sarde*, with fresh sardines, raisins, fennel and pine nuts and *spaghetti alla Norma* (named after the her-

At Charleston Le Terrazze in Mondello

oine in the opera by native son Bellini) with tomato, basil, fried aubergine and ricotta cheese.

Il Secondo is the main dish, which in Sicily is often fish, though chicken, veal, lamb and pork also appear on menus. *Pesce spada* (swordfish), caught in Sicilian waters, makes an appearance on menus all over the island, and is often grilled. *Tonno* (tuna) is also common, and is caught off the island as well. In the west, il cuscusu is a variation of Arab couscous, steamed in a fish broth.

Typical Sicilian *secondi* are *calamari ripieni alla griglia*, grilled squid filled with a stuffing of raisins, capers, garlic, pine nuts and anchovies; *cuscus*, a North African import common in western Sicily, served with a vegetable sauce; *cuscus con pesce*, the same dish topped with fish; *fritto misto*, a platter of fried clams, squid, cuttlefish, sardines and other seafood, depending (in a good restaurant) on what's fresh; and *involtini di pesce spada*, rolled swordfish cooked in breadcrumbs and oil. *Zuppa di pesce* is usually made with clams, mussels, squid and sometimes chunks of tuna or swordfish in a thick sauce of tomatoes, wine and olive oil.

The mountain pastures of the Madonie and Nebrodi produce exceptional lamb and pork. Beef is best stuffed and braised in tomato sauce or skewered and grilled *(involtini alla siciliana)*. *Scaloppine di vitello al Marsala* are veal escalopes cooked in Marsala wine (chicken and pork are also often prepared this way).

Contorni are vegetables, almost always ordered separately. While vegetables in antipasti are nearly always delicious, cooked vegetables and mixed salad are often a disappointment, the more so when you see the wonderful locally-grown produce in markets. Some common vegetables include *carciofi*, artichokes, *ceci*, chickpeas, *fagioli*, beans, usually white beans, *finocchio*, fennel, *melanzane*, eggplant (aubergines), *peperoni*, peppers, and *zucchini* (courgettes). Salads come in two basic varieties: *insalata verde*, a simple green salad, or *insalata mista*, mixed salad. You may also come across *arance e finocchio*, oranges and fennel salad – a legacy of the Arabs.

Frutti alla Martorana

Sicily is famed for its local produce and, at every social level, Sicilians enjoy good food and wine, often the simpler, the better. As anyone who has visited a caffè or *pasticceria* (confectioner) will have noticed, sweet decorated desserts, cakes and ice creams are particular favourites. There is an abundance of confections made with almonds too – almond orchards dot the countryside – but none more eye-catching, or sweeter, than the hand-made *frutti alla martorana*: garishly coloured fruits like peaches, oranges, grapes and prickly pears made from pure, sweet marzipan. These are a Sicilian speciality and take their name from the nuns of the convent at Palermo's La Martorana church, who first created them in 1233. The convent and the nuns are long gone but their marzipan extravagances live on.

Dolci are desserts. The Arab inheritance is reflected in spicy fruit jellies, sorbets and *cassata siciliana*, the cloyingly sweet sponge cake with almond paste and candied peel. The classic island favourites are *cannoli*, fried pastry tubes filled with ricotta and candied fruit and *frutti alla Martorana* (see box). *Crespelle di riso* are pancakes made with sweetened

Classic Sicilian dessert of *cannoli*

rice. Fruit, ricotta, honey, almonds and pistachio nuts often flavour cakes, ice cream and sorbets.

Drinks

Most Sicilians prefer to drink mineral water *(acqua minerale)*. *Acqua frissante, con gas,* or *gassata* all mean sparkling mineral water, *acqua naturale* or *non gassata* is still.

While canned soft drinks *(analcóliche)* are common don't overlook some of the more interesting alternatives that are available in Sicily. *Spremuta* is a fresh-squeezed juice, made with oranges *(arance)* or lemons *(limone)* grown on the island and a surefire remedy for the effects of summer heat; if you order a *spremuta di limone,* you will want to add sugar and water to your taste. A Sicilian speciality is *granita*, a sorbet made with crushed ice that is flavoured with the fresh juice of lemons, strawberries or other seasonal fruits or, sometimes sweetened coffee. Try mulberry *(mora)*, peach *(pesca)* or watermelon *(anguria)*.

Italian beer is excellent; ask for a *birra nazionale* and you will probably be served a bottle of Peroni or a Messina, which is brewed in Sicily. Many imported brands are also available, especially Kronenberg and Heineken. Draft beer (*birra alla spina*) is often imported and more expensive than you might expect.

Spirits are widely available, and are served neat, without ice, unless you ask for it (*ghiaccio*). It is customary for the bar to give you a complimentary selection of bite-size savouries with them. The island also makes several rather sticky and bitter, herbal tasting liqueurs, including Averna, which is made in Caltanissetta, and Fichera, from the slopes of Mount Etna. Some of the island's lemon harvest finds its way into *limoncello*, another syrupy after-dinner drink.

Wine

Sicilian wines have a great pedigree, dating back to Phoenician and Greek times, but have traditionally under-performed. With their prodigious amounts of sugar, they were dispatched north for blending, to bump up the strength of better-known wines. More recently, though, there has been a full-scale return to producing serious drinking wines, and to harnessing native grape varieties to that end. Good quality reds are made from the local Nero d'Avola grape variety; look out too for the dry red Cerasuolo di Vittoria from Ragusa province, the dry whites from Alcamo in the west and the up-and-coming new wines from the lava-enriched foothills of Etna.

Sicily's most famous wine – and long one of its most famous exports – is Marsala, a fortified wine comparable to

Wine resorts

Sicily has seen an increasing number of appealing wine estates where you can usually stay, dine or do a cookery or wine-tasting course. Just outside Alcamo, the Sirignano Wine Resort is a delightful organic estate run by the Marchese de Gregori. Guests stay in converted farm-workers' cottages and sample the superb wines over meals cooked by an outstanding chef.

port or sherry. It's been produced since the 18th century near the city on the southwestern coast from which it takes its name and is drunk as an aperitif or with/after dessert. A Marsala vergine rivals top sherries and ports. Restaurants in Marsala serve *Marsala all'uovo*, Marsala that has been blended with sugar and egg. If you find you like this particularly, as it is commercially produced you can find it in all shops and supermarkets.

Sweet elixirs, in fact, are something of a Sicilian speciality. Malvasia is another dessert wine made in the Aeolian Islands, and the island of

Sicilian reds are on the up

Pantelleria produces Moscato di Pantelleria Naturale, made from Zibibbo grapes that are fermented in the sun. Taormina produces vino alla Mandorla, a wine made from almonds.

Of course, Sicily also produces some excellent table wines. Many travellers may already be familiar with the island's red and white Corvos, which are exported around the world and are available throughout the island as well. Etna is produced from grapes grown on volcanic soil in the foothills of the volcano and is available as red, white or rosé. They tend to have a heavier and fruitier flavour. Some wines that are little known outside Sicily but are well worth looking for are Alcamo, from around Trápani, and Cerasuolo di Vittoria, from vineyards outside Ragusa.

USEFUL RESTAURANT TERMS

Here are a few terms that may enhance your dining experiences. Be bold – your efforts at speaking Italian will be much appreciated.

Buona sera. Good afternoon/evening.

Parla inglese? Do you speak English?

Aperto Open

Chiuso Closed

Prima colazione Breakfast

Pranzo Lunch

Cena Dinner

Avete un menu? Do you have a menu?

Vorrei... I would like...

Che cosa ci raccomanda What would you recommend

Quanto costa? How much is it?

Il conto, per favore. The bill, please.

Avete una tavola per una/due/tre/quattro persona/persone? Do you have a table for one/two/three/four people?

In addition to the regional specialities here are some common terms you are likely to encounter on Sicilian menus:

aglio garlic	**caffè** coffee
agnello lamb	**calamari** squid
baccalaru Sicilian for *baccalà*, salted cod	**ceci** chickpeas
basilica basil	**cipolle** onions
birra beer	**coniglio** rabbit
burro butter	**cozze** mussels
cacocciulo Sicilian for *carciofo*, artichoke	**fagioli** beans
	fegato liver
	finnochio fennel

formaggio cheese
frittata omelette
frutti di mare seafood
funghi mushrooms
gamberetti shrimp
insalata salad
leper hare
lumache snails
maiale pork
melanzane aubergine
pane bread
panna cream
patate potatoes
peperoni peppers
pesce fish

piccione pigeon
polipo octopus
pollo chicken
pomodori tomatoes
primo sale a sweet
   cheese
prosciutto ham
rognoni kidneys
spiedino skewers of meat
spinachi spinach
siccia Sicilian for *seppia*,
   cuttlefish
tè tea
uova eggs
vitello veal

SOME TYPICAL PASTAS

fettucine long, flat, narrow strips
fusilli spiral-shaped pasta
orecchiette ear-shaped pasta
pappardelle wide, short noodles
penne short tubes
tagliatelle flat egg noodles
vermicelli thin spaghetti

SOME COMMON PASTA SAUCES

aglio e olio with garlic, oil, light chilli
alla Norma with eggplant
alla panna with cream
arrabbiata hot tomato sauce, often with salted anchovies
bolognese meat sauce
napolitana with tomato and basil
pesto a mixture of basil, garlic, and pine nuts
vongole with clams, garlic and oil

PLACES TO EAT

Price for a two-course meal for one person, including a glass of wine and service charge:

€ below 20 euros   **€€** 20–30 euros
€€€ 30–40 euros   **€€€€** over 40 euros

PALERMO

Antica Focacceria San Francesco € *Via Paternostro 58, tel: (091) 320 264.* For a century and a half, this Palermo institution has been serving tasty, baked-on-the-premises focaccia bread and other rustic snacks from its high-ceilinged, marble-floored location. Closed Tuesday.

Cucina Papoff €€€ *Via Isidoro La Lumia 32, tel: (091) 586 460, www.cucinapapoff.com.* This welcoming little trattoria offers imaginative Sicilian cuisine in the vaults of an 18th century building. Try *fritella*, artichokes, fava beans and peas, followed by sword fish in citron and caper sauce, or go for *u maccu*, a creamy soup of fava beans with wild fennel. Dinner only, closed Sunday and August.

Osteria dei Vespri €€€ *Piazza Croce dei Vespri 6, tel: (091) 617 1631, www.osteriadeivespri.it.* This old tavern occupies the ex-coach house of the 18th century Palazzo Gangi on a lovely sheltered square with outdoor tables in summer. The cooking is creative Italian, with artfully presented dishes. Closed Sunday.

Pizzeria Bellini €–€€ *Piazza Bellini 6, tel: (091) 616 5691.* The setting is wonderful – in the arcades of a now defunct theatre and in the shadows of the Norman church of La Martorana – and the fare fits the bill when you are looking for homey Italian cooking.

Trattoria Primavera €€ *Piazza Bologni 4; tel: (091) 329 408.* Close to Quattro Canti, this is a lively, good-value trattoria. Choose from the extensive and colourful spread of antipasti, *pasta con le sarde* (fresh sardines), *pasta con i broccoli* and grilled calamari. The al fresco tables on the piazza are snapped up in summer. Closed all day Monday and Sunday dinner.

AEOLIAN ISLANDS (ISOLE EOLIE)

Il Canneto €€ *Via Roma 47, Stromboli; tel: (090) 986014.* Fish specialities here include *involtini di pesce spade* (swordfish rolled and stuffed), *spaghetti alla strombolana* (with anchovies and capers) and *tonno in agrodolce* (sweet and sour tuna). It's also open all day for coffee, *granite* and home-made patisserie. Closed Oct–May.

Il Filippino €€€€ *Piazza Municipio, Lípari, tel: (090) 981 1002.* A local favourite, the Filippino flows out onto a terrace overlooking the main town and harbour. Most of the menu, naturally, comes from the sea, and includes a famous *zuppa di pesce* (fish soup). Reservations recommended. Closed winter and Monday off season.

La Nassa €€ *Via G. Franza 41, Lípari; tel: (090) 9811 319, www.la nassavacanze.it.* Expect a warm welcome and genuine Aeolian cuisine in this delightful family-run restaurant. Local fish dominates the menu and full use is made of local produce: capers from Lípari, ricotta from Vulcano and Malvasia wine (served with home-made biscuits) from Salina. Closed Nov–Easter and Thur Apr-June.

AGRIGENTO

Trattoria dei Templi €€ *Via Panoramica dei Templi 15, tel: (0922) 403 110.* Fish dominates the menu at this vaulted rustic retreat near the temples. Fish of the day is always a good bet; or try raw marinated fish, prawn and *bottarga* (tuna roe), orange salad and *ragù* of red mullet with wild fennel. Very popular. Closed Sunday.

CATANIA

Costa Azzurra €€€ *Via de Cristoforo 4, Ógnina, tel: (095) 494 920.* This restaurant/pizzeria at Ógnina, just north of the central business district, is where Catanians come for excellent seafood meals. The views of the busy harbour are excellent, especially from the terrace. Closed Monday.

Osteria Antica Marina €€€ *Via Pardo 29, tel: (095) 348 197.* This atmospheric osteria is in the heart of the fish market so the fish couldn't be fresher. Choose from fish antipasti, pasta dishes with seafood sauces and plain grilled fish, charged by the kilo.

La Siciliana €€€ *Viale Marco Polo 52a, tel: (095) 376 400.* This is Sicilian cooking at its best, and in a charming garden setting. Specialities include roast lamb, *carpaccio* of fresh swordfish and imaginative vegetable dishes. Reservations required. Closed Monday and dinner Sunday.

Trattoria Il Mare €–€€ *Via S. Michele, 7, tel: (095) 317 024.* Just off the main shopping street this family-run, simply-furnished trattoria has first-class seafood. The fish antipasti is a real feast.

CEFALÙ

L'Antica Corte €€ *Cortile Pepe 7, tel: (0921) 423 228.* Fresh fish and pastas topped with seafood-based sauces are favourites on the menu in this old-town restaurant. The best seating is in the charming courtyard. Closed Thursday.

La Brace €€ *Via XXV Novembre 10, tel: (0921) 423 570.* Arches and a rough-hewn décor lend ambiance to this excellent-value eatery in the old town, near the Duomo. Booking here is essential. Closed Monday and Tuesday lunch.

ERICE

Monte San Giuliano €€ *Vicolo San Rocco 7, tel: (0923) 869 595.* A wide selection of Erice specialties, including couscous smothered in a rich fish broth, are served in the delightful terraced garden or cosy dining room. Closed Monday.

La Pentolaccia €–€€ *Via F.F. Guarnotti, 17; tel: (0923) 869 099.* In the centre of Erice, the restaurant occupies an old monastery where monks were famous for their pastries. Dishes here are all local, including fish and couscous specials. Good choice of local wines. Closed Tuesday and January and February.

MÓDICA

La Gazza Ladra €€€€ *Via Blandini 5, Modica Alta; tel: (0932) 755 655; www.ristorantelagazzaladra.it.* Michelin-starred restaurant is run by renowned chef Accursio Craparo in the boutique hotel Palazzo Failla. The cuisine has strongly Sicilian roots, with a nouvelle twist. Closed all day Monday and Sunday dinner.

La Locanda del Colonnello €€ *Vico Biscari 6, Piazza S. Teresa, Módica Alta; tel: (0932) 752423.* La Gazza Ladra's chef (see above) has opened an inn celebrating 'cucina povera' – rustic cuisine inspired by the simplest produce. Closed Wednesday.

NOTO

Trattoria del Carmine €€ *Via Ducezio 9, tel: (0935) 838 705.* Everything at this family-run trattoria is fresh and homemade. Regional specialities include seafood-based pastas and *coniglio alla stimpirate*, a traditional Sicilian rabbit dish. Closed Monday.

PIAZZA ARMERINA

Da Totò €€ *Via Mazzini 29, tel: (0935) 680 153.* A pleasant, family-run trattoria where the menu reflects the mountain setting, with an emphasis on game, rabbit and other meat dishes. Closed Monday in winter.

RAGUSA

Il Barocco €–€€ *Il Orfanotrofio 29, Ragusa Ibla, tel: (0932) 652 397, www.ilbarocco.it.* Within a palazzo, this popular restaurant/ pizzeria offers good house antipasti and a wide range of pastas. Excellent wine list. Closed Wednesday and two weeks August.

Il Duomo €€€–€€€€ *Via Capitano Boccheri 31, Ragusa Ibla, tel: (0932) 651 265, www.ristoranteduomo.it.* Arguably the best restaurant in Sicily, the elegant Duomo is renowned for intense, elaborate reinterpretations of Sicilian cuisine, as Baroque as Ibla itself. Closed Sunday and lunch Monday.

SIRACUSA

Archimede €€–€€€ *Via Gemellaro 8, Ortigia, tel: (0931) 697 01.* Long-established restaurant with garden and with a reputation for classic local dishes. Closed Sunday except Dec–Feb.

Da Mariano €€ *Viccolo Zuccolò 9, tel: (0931) 674 44, www.osteriada mariano.it.* Close to the Fonte Aretusa in Ortigia, this popular osteria serves authentic, good-value cuisine; the emphasis is on land-based cuisine from the Iblei mountains. Closed Tuesday.

Don Camillo €€€ *Via Maestranza 96, tel: (0931) 671 33.* An old Ortigia favourite serving wonderful variations of local specialties, including pasta with cuttlefish in its own ink or fresh tuna. The cellar has a choice of 700 wines. Closed Sunday, and November.

La Foglia €€ *Via Capodieci 21, tel: (0931) 662 33; www.lafoglia. it.* Owned by a sculptor and packed with paintings and eccentric decor, the trattoria is renowned as much for character as for cuisine.

TAORMINA

Al Duomo €€ *Vico Ebrei 1, tel: (0942) 625 656, www.ristoranteal duomo.it.* In the heart of the town this is an atmospheric, reliable restaurant with a rustic-chic interior and a sought-after terrace overlooking Piazza Duomo. Closed Wednesday.

Granduca €€€€ *Corso Umberto 170, tel: (0942) 24 983.* The charmingly cluttered, antiques-filled setting offers lovely views of the bay and excellent Sicilian dishes. Closed Tuesday.

Licchio's €€ *Via Patricio 10, tel: (0942) 625 327.* Almost alongside Porta Messina, this trattoria with a charming garden bustles with fashionable locals. The menu includes fish carpaccio, linguine with sea urchins, pizza and even curry. Booking recommended.

Vecchia Taormina €–€€ *Vico Ebrei 3, tel: (0942) 625 589.* Taormina's most popular casual eatery serves delicious pizza and other light fare. Closed Wednesday and lunch July–Aug.

A–Z TRAVEL TIPS

A Summary of Practical Information

A

ACCOMMODATION

Sicily has plentiful accommodation with prices similar to those on the mainland. The choice ranges from luxurious grand hotels in Palermo, Catania and Taormina and stylish new boutique hotels, to simple B&Bs and private rooms on farms. Accommodation in the interior is thinner on the ground, with the notable exception of the southeast where there is a swathe of special hotels in and around Siracusa, Ragusa, Módica and Scicli. Book ahead for popular resorts, such as Taormina, Cefalù and Siracusa, especially at Easter and in summer. The same applies to hotels on the offshore islands. Price differentials prevail between high, mid and low season. Many resorts close in winter; some hotels or *agriturismi* insist on half or full board in high season.

Agriturismi or farmstays have improved dramatically and are generally delightful and good value. To be labelled an *agriturismo* the property must have fewer than 30 beds, and earn most of its income from agricultural pursuits. Meals will more often than not feature homegrown ingredients. Tourist boards can provide information on farm stays, or consult www.agriturist.it. Villa rentals is now big business thanks to foreign villa-owners and design-conscious locals – as well as reputable villa specialists abroad.

I'd like a single/double bed. **Vorrei una camera singola/ matrimoniale** or **doppia.**
With bath/shower **Con bagno/doccia**
What is the price per night? **Qual è il prezzo per una notte?**

Many residents of the Aeolian and Egadi Islands rent rooms in their homes. Locals may offer you accommodation as you step off the ferry; alternatively ask at a bar or local travel agency and look for signs announcing *camere libre* (rooms for rent).

AIRPORTS *(Aeroporti)*

Sicily currently has three international airports: Palermo (Falcone-Borsellini), Catania (Fontanarossa) and Trápani (Birgi). A new airport, Comiso, close to Ragusa, is complete but has yet to open. London and other major European cities have direct flights to Sicily. From New York there are twice weekly non-stop flights to Palermo operated by Eurofly/Meridiana (www.eurofly.com). Other flights from North America, and from Australia and New Zealand, go direct to Rome, Milan or a major hub elsewhere in Europe, and continue to Palermo or Catania from there.

Palermo's **Aeroporto Falcone Borsellino** (www.gesap.it) is 30km (18 miles) west of the city at Punta Raisi. Buses run every half hour from 5.30am to the time of the last arrival of the day to Palermo's Piazza Politeama and the central train station. The journey time is 45 minutes to an hour. The Trinacria Express train service, which also runs every half hour from the airport to the central station, takes 55 minutes and is a fraction cheaper than the bus. A taxi to Palermo centre costs €40.

Catania's **Aeroporto Fontanarossa** (www.aeroporto.catania.it) is 5km (3 miles) south of the city. Buses leave from outside the terminal for the 20-minute trip to Piazza Stesicoro in the centre of the city and to Stazione Centrale, departing roughly every 20 minutes from 5.30am to midnight. Buses from the airport also make connections to Siracusa, Ragusa, Taormina and many other cities in eastern Sicily, as well as Palermo. A taxi to the centre costs €25-€30.

Trápani-Birgi's Aeroporto **Vincenzo Florio** (www.airgest.it), used by low-cost carriers, is 15kms (9 miles) southeast of Trápani. AST buses link the airport to the town every half hour, taking 25 minutes, with connections to Palermo, Agrigento and Marsala. Terravision coaches (www.terravision.eu) to Palermo link up with Ryanair flights.

When is the next plane to…? **A che ora parte il prossimo aereo per…?**
I would like a ticket for… **Vorrei un biglietto per…**
Please take these bags to the train/bus/taxi.
Mi porti queste valige fino al treno/all'autobus/ al taxi, per favore.

B

BUDGETING FOR YOUR TRIP

When determining your budget, think of Palermo and Taormina and the rest of Sicily as two separate entities. Hotels in Palermo can be as expensive as those in Rome, and lodgings in Taormina are on par with those in Positano, Italy's popular resort; accommodation elsewhere in Sicily is moderate in terms of cost. In Palermo you can expect to pay €180 to €300 for standard double accommodation. Outside of Palermo or Taormina, you can probably find a similar room for €100 to €200.

You can usually enjoy a three-course meal for two (excluding wine) for about €50–60; a lunch of pizza or a salad for two will be about half that. Entry fees to museums and archaeological sites average €5. EU citizens over 65 or under 18 are allowed free entry to most sights, and those of 18–25 get a 50 percent discount. Passport, ID or driving licence is required.

C

CAMPING

Camping is permitted only in designated sites, of which there are about 90 in Sicily. Most are on the coast and on the Aeolian and Egadi Islands. Tourist boards include campgrounds in their accommodation listings; alternatively, go to www.camping.it.

CAR HIRE (Autonoleggio)

Most major companies such as Avis, Hertz and Europcar have outlets at the airports but it is usually cheaper to book in advance. Car rental costs from around €270 per week for a small car. 'Inclusive' prices do not generally include personal accident insurance or insurance against damage to windscreens, tyres and wheels. For renting, the minimum age is usually 25. Drivers must present their own national driving licence or one that is internationally recognised. Credit card imprints are taken as a deposit and are usually the only form of payment acceptable.

CLIMATE

Sicily enjoys good weather year-round, with mild winters and hot summers. The only extremes you can expect are in July and August, when daytime temperatures of 40°C (95°F) are not unusual. The southern coast is the warmest place on the island, and it is often buffeted by hot sirocco winds that blow in off the Sahara. November and December can be rainy and expect the occasional shower until March. Spring arrives early and the island is unusually pleasant at this time because wildflowers bloom everywhere. Below are average temperatures in Palermo, accurate for most of the island except in the cooler mountainous interior and on the southern coast in the summer.

	J	F	M	A	M	J	J	A	S	O	N	D
°C	10.5	10.5	13	16	18.5	23	25.5	25	23	20	17	12.5
°F	52	52	55	61	73	78	77	73	68	62	62	56

CLOTHING

Bring light clothing and a hat during the hot summer months. In spring and autumn, you will need a jacket or sweater for the evenings. Winters, particularly in mountainous central areas, can be cold so bring warm clothes and waterproofs. Shorts are acceptable but bathing attire off the beach is often frowned upon, and wearing miniskirts, skimpy shorts or shoulderless garments in churches is likely to cause offence. At the largest, most-visited churches a guard is posted at the front door to check for immodest attire.

CRIME AND SAFETY

Petty crime against tourists is fairly common in Sicily, especially pick-pocketing and purse- and jewellery-snatching. Car theft is also fairly common, as is the theft of goods from within a parked car. Leave passports, jewellery, large amounts of cash, credit cards you are not using and other valuables in the hotel safe (many hotels provide them in the rooms; if not, ask to check in valuables at the desk). Keep a copy of your passport and other valuable documents separately in case you need to replace them. Be particularly vigilant at markets, street festivals and other occasions where large crowds congregate.

Never leave valuables in view within your car; whenever possible, park in an attended lot (most archaeological sites and other attractions have them). To protect yourself against Vespa-riding bandits, who snatch bags while whizzing by at high speed, carry your bag so it faces away from the street.

If you are robbed, report it as soon as possible to the local police. You will need a copy of the declaration in order to claim on your insurance.

I want to report a theft. **Voglio denunciare un furto.**
My wallet/passport/ticket has been stolen. **Mi hanno rubato il portafoglio/il passaporto/il biglietto.**

D

DISABLED TRAVELLERS

Sicily is one of the worst places in Italy for disabled travellers to get around. Most churches and sites have steps, and few of the museums and archaeological sites have wheelchair access. Given the challenges it is wisest to book through a specialised tour operator or travel agency who can offer customised tours and itineraries, eg Flying Wheels Travel (www.flyingwheelstravel.com) and Accessible Journeys (www.disabilitytravel.com).

DRIVING

A car in Sicily is a great help for exploring the island, though in cities like Palermo, Catania or Siracusa, it is easier and less nerve-wracking to use public transport or taxis. The network of roads has much improved though you can still expect potholes even on some of the major roads. A system of mainly toll-free motorways (*autostrade*) crosses parts of the island, linking the main cities. Elsewhere, roads can be quite slow-going, especially in the mountainous regions. The main frustrations of driving in Sicily are negotiating town centres (which often have complex one-way systems and poor signing to the centre), finding parking places in town centres and keeping your cool with fellow motorists who drive fast and frequently recklessly.

Curva pericolosa Dangerous curve
Deviazione Detour (diversion)
Divieto di sorpasso No passing (overtaking)
Divieto di sosta No stopping
Lavori in corso Men working (road works)
Pericolo Danger
Rallentare Slow down
Senso vietato/unico No entry/one-way street
Vieto l'ingresso No entry
Zona pedonale Pedestrian zone
Zona traffico limita Limited traffic zone

Rules and Regulations. The speed limit on motorways is 130km/h (80mph), secondary roads is 90km/h (55mph); in towns, it's 50km/h

(30mph). Drive on the right, overtake on the left. At intersections and traffic circles (roundabouts), traffic on the right has the right of way. Speeding and other traffic offences are subject to heavy on-the-spot fines. The use of hand-held mobiles while driving is prohibited. The blood alcohol limit is 0.08 percent, and police occasionally make random breath tests. Lights must be used on all out-of-town roads.

Breakdowns and Assistance. In case of an accident or breakdown, dial 113 (general emergency) or the Automobile Club of Italy on 116. Roadside phones are placed at frequent intervals along major roads.

Parking. Historic centres are often inaccessible to cars, other than those of residents, though visitors staying at hotels with parking facilities are allowed access. Many Sicilian cities and towns have municipal parking lots and garages, denoted by a white 'P' on a blue background, at the fringes of their historic centers; use these whenever possible.

Fuel. Petrol (*benzina*) is readily available and there are many 24-hour stations with self-service dispensers that accept euro notes and credit cards.

Driver's licence **Patente**
Car registration papers **Libretto di circolazione**
Green insurance card **Carte verde**
Can I park here? **Posso parcheggiare qui?**
Are we on the right road for…? **Siamo sulla strada giusta per…?**
Fill the tank, please, with… **Per favore, faccia il pieno de…**
I've had a breakdown. **Ho avuto un guasto.**
There's been an accident. **C'è stato un incidente.**

E

ELECTRICITY

220V/50Hz is standard. Visitors from other countries may require an adaptor (*una presa complementare*), and those from North America will need a converter as well. Connections are either two or three round-pins. Adaptors can be found locally, but it is wiser to carry an international adaptor. Better hotels often have special outlets for some North American appliances.

EMBASSIES AND CONSULATES

In Rome:
Australian Embassy: Via Antonio Bosio 5; tel: 06 852 721; www.italy.embassy.gov.au
Canadian Embassy: Via Zara 30, tel: 06 8544 43937; www.canada.it
Irish Embassy: Piazza Campitelli 3; tel: 06 697 9121; www.ambasciata-irlanda.it
UK Embassy: Via XX Settembre 80a; tel: 06 4220 0001; www.britain.it
US Embassy: Via Vittorio Veneto 121; tel: 06 46741; www.usembassy.it

EMERGENCIES

The general emergency number is 113. Call 112 for police, 115 for fire and 118 for an ambulance. For road assistance dial 116.

Please, can you place an emergency call for me to the…? **Per favore, può fare me una telefonata d'emergenza…?**
police **alla polizia**
Fire! **Al fuoco!**
fire brigade **ai pompieri**
ambulance **ambulanza**
hospital **al'ospedale**

G

GAY AND LESBIAN TRAVELLERS

Attitudes are fairly relaxed and gay magazines are sold at most newsstands. Taormina is still the focus for the native and foreign gay community. Its gay bars come and go. Consult Arci-gay, the national gay rights organisation, www.arcigay.it, or contact the Palermo branch (tel: 349 884 5809; email palermo@arcigay.it). To access bars and discos, you need to join the association, with a special membership card for foreigners.

GETTING THERE

By Air. Major European cities have direct flights to Sicily. From the UK direct services are operated by British Airways from Gatwick to Catania; low-cost carrier Easyjet flies to Catania and Palermo from Gatwick, Ryanair from Stansted to Palermo and from Luton to Trápani. From New York there are twice weekly flights direct to Palermo operated by Eurofly/Meridiana (www.eurofly.com). Other flights from North America, and from Australia and New Zealand, fly to Rome or Milan or a major hub elsewhere in Europe and continue to Palermo or Catania from there.

By Rail. The Italian mainland is linked to Sicily by train, with Milan, Rome and Naples the best connecting stations to the south. Unfortunately, the great improvements in the Italian rail system do not extend to Sicily, and the overnight sleeper service from Sicily to northern Italy has been cancelled.

There is a daily service between Rome and Palermo, Catania and Siracusa. At the crossing from Villa San Giovanni on the Italian peninsula the train carriages are shunted into the ferry, and then shunted off again at Messina. Palermo's main station is Stazione Centrale. Always book a seat for long-distance travel. Credit card bookings can be made online (www.trenitalia.com) or go through any local travel agent.

By Sea. Ferries link Sicily with Naples, Genova (Genoa), Salerno and Civitavecchia in Italy and with Cagliari in Sardinia; there are also links with Tunis and Malta. Hydrofoils (*aliscafi*) operate between Sicily and its smaller islands (see page 132). Sicily can be combined with Malta on a two-island holiday using Virtu Ferries (www.virtuferries.com).

Ferry tickets can be booked online (though there is no need for the Messina/Villa San Giovanni crossing). The main operators are SNAV (www.snav.it), Grandi Navi Veloci (www.gnv.it), Tirrenia (www.tirrenia.it) and Grimaldi (www.grimaldi-lines.com). There are cabins on the longer routes, and these must be booked well in advance for high summer. Remember that sailing schedules are prone to change, especially in winter months when the seas can turn rough.

By Car. Driving to Sicily from the UK takes 24 hours. Even from Rome it is a good seven hours to Villa San Giovanni in Calabria, where you cross to Sicily. To bring a car into Italy you will need a current driving licence and valid insurance. You must carry your driving licence, car registration, insurance documents and passport with you at all times when driving. You are also required to carry a triangular warning sign and a visibility vest.

GUIDES AND TOURS *(Guide E Viaggi)*

Guides are readily available in Sicily's cities and at its archaeological sites to provide tours in English though prices are high for small groups. The Italian government tourist office, local tourist offices, travel agencies and hotels can provide lists. The hop-on hop-off sightseeing bus (www.palermo.city-sightseeing.it) with multilingual commentary, is a popular way of getting around in Palermo and one route goes as far as Monreale.

I would like an English-speaking guide. **Ho bisogno di una guida chi parla inglese.**

H

HEALTH AND MEDICAL CARE

Residents of the EU should carry with them the European Health Insurance Card or ehic (available in the UK from post offices or online at www.nhs-ehic.org.uk), which entitles them to free medical treatment within the EU. This only covers medical care, not emergency repatriation costs or additional expenses. It is therefore advisable and for non-EU residents, essential, to have travel insurance to cover all eventualities. You will often be asked to pay for treatment up front, so keep all receipts for reimbursement. In many areas in summer there is a *Guardia Medica Turistica* (tourist emergency medical service) which functions 24 hours a day. Details are available from pharmacies, tourist offices, hotels and local newspapers.

Pharmacies *(farmacie)* have green cross signs above the entrance; in each town, one stays open late and on Sundays on a rotating basis. The after-hour locations for the month are posted in all pharmacies. For serious cases or emergencies, dial 118 for an ambulance or head for the *Pronto Soccorso* (Accident and Emergency) of the local hospital.

I need a doctor/dentist. **Ho bisogno di un medico/ dentista.**
I have a stomach ache. **Ho mal di stomaco.**
I have sunstroke. **Ho una colpo di sole.**

Water is considered safe to drink, though like most Italians, Sicilians prefer bottled water.

L

LANGUAGE

Many Sicilians speak Italian and Sicilian, which is a rich blend of Italian and the languages of the various powers who have invaded the island over the centuries; Arabic, French, and Spanish words appear regularly. English is spoken in hotels and restaurants, but once you venture off the tourist track, prepare to communicate in Italian.

Here are some basic tips:

a as in *father*
e as in *egg*
i as *e* in *eat*
o as in *ostracize*
u as *oo* in *mood*
c before *e* and *i* is pronounced *ch*, as in *church*. Otherwise, *c* and *ch* are pronounced *k*, as in *cane*.
g before *e* and *i* is pronounced *j*, as in *gin*. Before other letters, *g* is hard, as in *gun*.
Most feminine words end in *a*, plural *e*, and most masculine words end in *o*, plural *i*. *La* is the feminine article, *il* the masculine.

Some basic words and phrases:

Good morning/good afternoon. **Buon giorno.** bwon JOARno
Please. **Per favore.** pair fahVOAray
Thank you. **Grazie.** GRAAseeay
yes/no **sì/no** see/no
Excuse me. **Mi scusi.** mi skoozee
Where is…? **Dovè…?** doaVAI…?
I don't understand. **Non capisco.** noan kahpeeskoa
open **aperto** ahPAIRtoe
closed **chiuso** keeOOso

Days of the week:

Monday **lunedì**
Tuesday **martedì**
Wednesday **mercoledì**
Thursday **giovedì**
Friday **venerdì**
Saturday **sabato**
Sunday **domenica**

Numbers

one **uno**	five **cinque**	nine **nove**
two **due**	six **sei**	ten **diece**
three **tre**	seven **sette**	hundred **cento**
four **quattro**	eight **otto**	

M

MAPS

A good map is handy when you go off the beaten track into Sicily's mountainous interior. Maps of Sicily by Michelin Italia (www.viamichelin.com) are excellent, as are those published by the Touring Club Italiano (www.touringclub.it); you can find them in most bookstores. Sicilian tourist offices can supply free maps of towns and resorts of variable quality.

MEDIA

English-language newspapers are available at newsstands in major towns and resorts the day after publication. *The International Herald-Tribune* is widely available. The main Italian papers, *Corriere della Sera* and *La Repubblica*, publish southern editions but the local dailies are more popular. *Il Giornale di Sicilia*, Palermo's paper, covers western Sicily and includes practical listings. *La Sicilia*, Catania's main paper, also has provincial supplements for Siracusa, Ragusa and Enna. Even small hotels now often provide English-language television news channels.

MONEY

Currency. The unit of currency in Italy is the euro, written as €. Notes are denominated in 5, 10, 20, 50, 100 and 500; coins in 1 and 2 euros and 1, 2, 5, 10, 20 and 50 cents.
Currency Exchanges. Changing money in a bank can be time-

consuming, but the rates are generally better than in exchange offices. Exchange offices *(cambios)*, found in most towns, have longer opening hours. Main post offices and train stations usually have currency-exchange facilities.

Traveller's Cheques and Credit Cards. Both are widely accepted in hotels, restaurants and the larger shops though most establishments give an unfavourable exchange rate on traveller's cheques; you are better off cashing them at a currency exchange and paying in cash. Visa and Master Card are the most widely accepted credit cards, and many establishments do not take American Express cards.

○

OPENING HOURS

Museums and monuments throughout Sicily are remaining open longer than they once did, often seven days a week and into the early evening. Even so, hours vary widely. Smaller museums may open mornings only, or mornings and just for a couple of afternoons a week. Some are closed on Monday, and also Sunday afternoon. Most churches open early, around 7am or 8am for Mass, close at noon, then open again for two or three hours at 4pm or 5pm; but don't be surprised to find churches closed for ongoing restorations, and that major sites can close without warning. Some museums and archaeological sites are closed on Mondays. Local tourist boards can provide current opening times for sights in a particular town or region.

Banks. Generally open Mon–Fri 8.30am–1.30pm. Some are open in the afternoon 2.30–4pm or 3–4.30pm.

Shops and businesses. Opening times are Mon–Sat 8 or 9am–1pm and 4–7.30pm, but many non-food shops close on Monday and, with the exception of supermarkets, food shops usually close on Wednesday. In Taormina the shops are open daily.

Restaurants. Open 1–3pm or 3.30pm for lunch and from 8–10.30pm for dinner (closed one day a week).

P

POLICE *(polizia)*

There are three kinds of police in Italy: *vigili urbani*, who deal with petty crime, traffic, parking and other day-to-day matters; *carabinieri*, the highly trained national force who handle serious crime and civilian unrest, protect government figures and perform other high-profile tasks; and *polizia stradale*, who patrol the roadways. Any of these forces may answer a 113 emergency call, though the carabinieri have their own emergency number, 112.

Where's the nearest police station? **Dovè il più vicino posto di polizia?**

POST OFFICES

Post offices are open from 8am–1.30pm Mon–Sat, and in major cities the main post office is usually open seven days a week from 8am–7.30pm. If you want something to arrive with alacrity, consider using the more expensive Posta Prioritaria. Stamps can be bought in tobacconists *(tabacchi)* too.

I would like a stamp for this letter/postcard. **Desidero un francobollo per questa lettera/cartolina.**
Airmail **Via aerea**

PUBLIC HOLIDAYS

Sicily celebrates local festivals throughout the year (see page 95), and all of the national holidays as well. These are:
1 January New Year's Day (Capodanno)
6 January Epiphany (Befana)
Spring Easter Sunday and Monday (Pasqua)

25 April Liberation Day (Anniversario della Liberazione)
1 May Labour Day (Festa del Lavoro)
15 August Ferragosto and Assumption Day
1 November All Saints Day (Ognisanti)
8 December Day of the Immaculate Conception (Immacolata)
25 December Christmas (Natale)
26 December St Stephen's Day (Santo Stefano)

R

RELIGION

Like the rest of Italy, Sicily is predominantly Roman Catholic, and Sicilians are more devout than Italians elsewhere. The church, in fact, is
still a major part of the community, even in the cities – note the many
religious festivals that Sicilians celebrate (see page 95). Shoulderless garments and skimpy shorts should be avoided when visiting churches.

T

TELEPHONE *(telefono)*

For calls within Italy, telephone numbers must be preceded by the
full area code even if the call is made within the same district. When
phoning abroad form Italy dial 00, then the country code, followed
by the city or area code and the number (omitting any initial 0).
International dialling codes are 1 for the US and Canada, 44 for the
UK, 353 for the Republic of Ireland, 61 for Australia, 64 for New
Zealand. Hotels slap very large surcharges on long-distance calls.

Public phones Public phones, which are not as widespread as they
used to be, take credit cards or phone cards *(scheda telefonica)*, available
at tobacco shops and newsagents. Instructions are given in English.

Mobile (Cell) Phones Check the international roaming rates with
your provider prior to departure, and whether your phone can receive and make calls in Italy. Roaming rates are generally high and

if you are making a lot of calls or staying for some time it may be worth purchasing a SIM 'pay as you go' card, available at shops of the main providers or at the post office.

TIME ZONES

Like the rest of Italy, Sicily is on Central European Time, that is one hour ahead of Greenwich Mean Time (gmt). Italy switches to daylight saving time on the last Sunday in March and reverts to standard time on the last Sunday in October.

New York	**Sicily**	Jo'burg	Sydney	Auckland
7am	**noon**	1pm	9pm	11pm

TIPPING

In Italy a service charge of 10–15 percent is usually built into the bill, though a little extra for good service is always appreciated. At a bar, it is customary to leave a coin or two on the counter for a barman. Tip bellhops one euro per bag. To tip a taxi driver, simply round up the total.

TOILETS *(bagni)*

Public restrooms can be hard to find, and when you do locate one, you usually have to pay to use it. Toilets in cafés and bars can be used by the public but buying a drink at the same time will be appreciated. The mens' restroom is designated by *uomini* or *signori*, the ladies' by *donne* or *signore*. Major sites now have reasonable facilities but those in train and bus stations are not always well maintained.

Is it possible to use the bathroom? **Posso usare il bagno?**
Where are the toilets? **Dove sono i gabinetti?**

TOURIST INFORMATION

An office of the Italian National Tourist Office (ENIT) in your home country can supply listings of accommodation throughout Sicily and a wealth of other information. Locations are:

UK: 1 Princes Street, London W1B 2AY, tel: 0207 408-1254.

Canada: 110 Yonge Street, Suite 503, M5C 1T4, Toronto (Ontario), tel: 416-925-4882.

US: 630 Fifth Avenue, Suite 1965, New York, NY 10111, tel: 212-245-5618; 500 N. Michigan Avenue, Suite 506, Chicago, IL 60611, tel: 312-644-0996; 10850 Wilshire Boulevard, Suite 725, Los Angeles, CA 90024, tel: 310-820-1898.

The website for all of the above is: www.enit.it

Within Sicily most of the main tourist offices will have staff who speak foreign languages, but this is often not the case with smaller information offices. If you can't find a tourist office try a travel agency or local tour operator as these can be good sources of advice.

Agrigento: Via Empedocle, 73, tel: 0922 20391.

Catania: Via Vittorio Emanuele II 172, tel: 095 742557, www.turismo.catania.it.

Cefalù: Corso Ruggero 77, tel: 0921 421050.

Lípari: Corso Vittorio Emanuele, 202, tel: 090 9880095.

Palermo (city and province): Piazza Castelnuovo 34, tel: 091 605 8351, www.palermotourism.com.

Siracusa: Via Roma 31, Ortigia, tel: 800 055500; and Via Maestranza 33, tel: 0931 464255.

Taormina: Palazzo Corvaja, Piazza Santa Caterina, tel: 0942 23243.

Trápani: Info Point, Via San Grancesco d'Assisi 27, tel: 0923 8068008, www.apt.trapani.it.

TRANSPORT

Coach and Bus

Fast bus services, operated by various different companies, link Sicily's main towns and offer relatively speedy access to the interior and the south. Generally speaking, coaches are more reliable and quicker than trains, but they cost more. City buses have a flat fare and tickets are valid for 75 minutes, including change of bus routes. Services are limited on Sundays, and in many cases, after the late afternoon. Bus tickets, available from bars, tobacconists, and from machines at bus terminals and metro stations, must be validated in the machine on the bus. Tourist offices can provide bus schedules and fare information.

Ferries and Hydrofoils

Aeolian Islands: Ferries and hydrofoils run regularly from Milazzo on the northern coast near Messina. Boats run year round to all the islands with the most extensive service in the summer (in peak season there are up to 11 hydrofoils a day to Lípari and Vulcano, and six a day to Salina). There are direct ferries to the islands several times a week, but all can best be reached through Lípari. Off-season boats can be cancelled due to inclement weather.

Egadi Islands: Trápani on the western coast is the port for ferries and hydrofoils to the Egadi Islands (Favignana, Lévanzo and Maréttimo) and Pantelleria.

Ferries to the islands are mainly operated by Siremar (www.siremar.it) and Uscita Lines (www.usticalines.it).

Rail

Trains are operated by Italian State Railways, Ferrovie dello Stato (www.trenitalia.com). The rail system in Sicily is cheap but slow and not really convenient for seeing all of the island. The east of the island is better linked than the west. Messina is well linked to both Palermo and Catania, and all trains to Italy pass through its port in order to cross the Strait of Messina by ferry. Catania is linked with the major cities (though trains take twice as long from here to Palermo as the coach) and is the starting point of the Ferrovia Circumetnea, the narrow-gauge train that calls at all villages around Mount Etna on a circular route. Seat reservations are obligatory on the faster Intercity services. Tickets for all trains must be stamped in the yellow machines on the platforms before boarding the train.

Failure to do so can incur a hefty on-the-spot fine.

Taxi

In cities, taxis are best telephoned or found at taxi ranks in the main squares of the larger towns. Licensed taxis are white, with a Taxi sign on the roof, and have a meter which should be turned on at the start of the journey. Beware of touts without meters who may approach you at airports and large train stations.

Palermo: Radio Taxi: tel: 091 513311; 091 513198.

Catania: Radio Taxi: tel: 095 330966.

When is the next bus/train to…? **Quando parte il prossimo autobus/treno per…?**
one way **andata**
roundtrip **andata e ritorno**
first/second class **prima/seconda classe**
What's the fare to…? **Qual è la tariffa per…?**

V

VISAS AND ENTRY REQUIREMENTS

Citizens of EU countries need only a valid passport or an identity card to enter Italy. Citizens of the US, Canada, Australia, New Zealand and South Africa need only a valid passport, though a special visa or resident permit is required for stays of more than 90 days. To facilitate the replacement process in case you lose your passport while travelling, photocopy the first page of your passport twice; leave one copy at home and keep another with you, but separately from the passport.

EU regulations now allow for the free exchange of goods for personal use between member countries. For residents of non-EU countries, the following restrictions apply:

IVA. A Value Added Tax of around 20 percent is added to all purchases in Italy. Residents of non-EU countries can claim a refund for part of this tax on purchases of more than about €155 at stores participating in the VAT-refund scheme. The store will issue you a refund document, which you can redeem at the airport once you present your receipt to customs and have it stamped.

W

WEBSITES AND INTERNET ACCESS

Useful sites are:

www.enit.it Italian government Tourist Board, covering all of Italy.
www.regione.sicilia.it/turismo official Sicilian tourist website, not always up to date. Go to 'La Sicilia per il Turista' on the home page for tourist information with an English version.
www.yourwaytosicilia.com official Sicilian tourist office website.
www.parks.it Italian parks and reserves (then consult Sicily).
www.bestofsicily.com packed with information on the island; strong on culture.
www.thinksicily.com villas in Sicily, plus a useful guide to the island.
www.bed-and-breakfast-sicilia.it wide choice of B&Bs, guest houses, holiday homes and apartments.

Accessing the Internet: internet cafés and cheap hole-in-the-wall Internet/Telephone offices are widespread in the larger towns. Some hotels have a computer available for guests and many now have Wi-Fi, either throughout the hotel, or in public areas, sometimes free but more often than not with a charge. Wi-Fi hotspots in public areas are scant in Sicily.

Y

YOUTH HOSTELS

There are very few hostels in Sicily. For information and free reservations contact the Hostelling International Italian affiliate, Associazione Italiana Alberghi per la Gioventù (aig), www.aighostels.com.

Recommended Hotels

Sicily has over 500 hotels, classified from 1-star to 5-star de luxe. Bed and Breakfast accommodation is now widespread and often provides better value than, say, a 2-star hotel. The selective list of hotels below stand out either for setting, ambience, food, good value – or, if you are lucky, all four. Reservations are essential almost anywhere in Sicily from Easter through to September.

The symbols below are a rough indication of what you can expect to pay for a double room with bathroom, including breakfast in high season. A few hotels insist on half board during the summer. Off season, rates are usually reduced; if not, request a *sconto* (discount).

Note that hotels in some of the larger cities are now charging a hotel tax of €2–€4 per person for the first five consecutive nights.

€	less than 110 euros
€€	110–180 euros
€€€	180–300 euros
€€€€	over 300 euros

PALERMO

BB22 €€ *Palazzo Pantelleria, Largo Cavalieri di Malta 22; tel: (091) 611 1610; www.bb22.it.* This unique B&B has an excellent location, in the historic centre, tucked behind San Domenico and close to the Vucciria market. The seven guest rooms are individually furnished, all with designer chic. All rooms have en-suite bathrooms and free WiFi.

Centrale Palace Hotel €€€€€ *Corso Vittorio Emanuele 327, tel: (091) 336 666, www.centralepalacehotel.it.* In a 17th-century palace just a few steps from the Quattro Canti. With its good-sized guest rooms, handsome furnishings and excellent service, the Centrale has also become one of Palermo's better and more stylish hotels.

Grand Hotel et des Palmes €€–€€€€ *Via Roma 398, tel: (091) 602 8111, www.grandhoteldespalmes.com.* Palermo's famous grand hotel retains its grandeur and charm, making it easy to understand why

Palermo society still meets here and celebrities continue to check in (one of the first guests of note was Richard Wagner). The public rooms are ornate and beautifully maintained. If you don't like the room you are given, ask to see several others because all are different; the best are those that retain their high ceilings and fin de siècle furnishings.

Tonic €€ *Via Mariano Stabile 126, tel: (091) 781 6844, www.hoteltonic. it.* One of the best city bargain lodgings, this 3-star is centrally located with plainly furnished rooms, friendly staff and good buffet breakfasts.

Villa Igiea Hilton €€€–€€€€ *Salita Belmonte 43, tel: (091) 631 2111, www.villaigiea.hilton.comt.* This grand art nouveau villa, on the sea at Acquasanta, provides a perfect retreat in surroundings that were once home to the Florio family (of tuna and wine fame). The gardens and sea views are lovely, and amenities include a beach club, boat trips, swimming pool, tennis courts and shuttle bus service to Palermo.

AROUND PALERMO

Mondello Palace €€€–€€€€ *Viale Principe di Scalea, Mondello, tel: (091) 450 001, www.mondellopalacehotel.it.* Palermo's favourite seaside retreat is the setting for this well-equipped resort, within easy reach of the city centre but offering a pool, beach and other amenities. Rooms are good-sized, mainly with sea views. Reserve well ahead in summer.

CEFALÙ

Baia del Capitano €€€ *Contrada Mazzaforno, Cefalù, tel: (0921) 420 005, www.baiadelcapitano.it.* This low-key resort is 5km (3 miles) west of Cefalù, set in gardens and olive groves above the sea. There's a pool and tennis courts, and the beach is accessible on foot or by the free hotel shuttle. Closed Nov–Feb.

La Giara €€ *Via Veterani 40, tel: (0921) 421 562, www.hotel-lagiara. it.* The setting, right in the middle of the old city, is one of the main draws of this small, family-run hotel. The indoors, while not luxurious, is pleasing and quite comfortable. A terrace on the roof provides an ideal view over red tile roofs and the duomo.

Riva del Sole €€€ *Lungomare Giardina 25, tel: (0921) 421 230, www. rivadelsole.com.* The main attraction of this hotel is the location, just outside the old town, and overlooking the promenade and beach. Guest rooms provide solid comfort and pleasant furnishings, as well as sea views from the majority. Closed November.

USTICA

Clelia €€ *Via Sindaco 29, tel: (091) 844 9039, www.hotelclelia.it.* On the main square with its own excellent trattoria serving local dishes, this is the oldest pensione in town. The hotel also has a number of holiday houses sleeping between two and four people.

AEOLIAN ISLANDS (ISOLE EOLIE)

Diana Brown, € *Vico Himera 3, Lípari, tel: (090) 981 2584, www. dianabrown.it.* Run by a South African-Sicilian couple, this B&B on a tiny street five minutes' walk from the port has 12 recently refurbished rooms (5 with self-catering facilities) and a lovely roof terrace. Guests receive a friendly welcome – and there's always help at hand if you want to plan the day's activities.

Gattopardo Park €€ *Viale Diana, 98055 Lípari, tel: (090) 981 1035, www.gattopardoparkhotel.com.* Located near the centre of Lípari, this Italianate villa and surrounding bungalows are set in lush gardens, and guest quarters are pleasantly rustic.

Raya €€€€ *Via San Pietro, Panarea, tel: (090) 983 013, www.hotelraya. it.* This is considered a cult hotel, at once contemporary and timeless, set on the most chic island in the Aeolians yet still laidback and effortlessly charming. A favourite amongst celebrities.

TAORMINA

Mazzarò Sea Palace €€€€ *Via Nazionale 147, Mazzarò, tel: (0942) 612 111, www.mazzaroseapalace.it.* One of the most luxurious of the hotels that spread along the sea outside Taormina, the Mazzarò Sea Palace is a distinctive modern property that climbs down a hillside from the coast road. Rooms are spacious, stylishly furnished and face the sea and private beach from large terraces.

San Domenico Palace €€€€ *Piazza San Domenico 5, tel: (0942) 613 111, www.amthotels.it.* A 15th-century monastery manages to retain its austere Renaissance charm while housing one of Italy's most famous and luxurious hotels. Rooms occupy the monks' cells (which have been refitted to provide more spacious accommodation), and are richly furnished; many afford sweeping views along the coast. The chapel is now a bar, while the cloisters remain a peaceful retreat. A swimming pool is set amid the lush gardens and there are two gastronomic restaurants.

Villa Belvedere €€€ *Via Bagnoli Croci 79, tel: (0942) 23791, www. villabelvedere.it.* This lovely hotel is located on a hillside just above Taormina's public gardens, with fabulous views (hence the name). It's set amid its own semi-tropical gardens that surround a lavish swimming pool. Many of the comfortable rooms have balconies, and those in the villa that forms the older section of the hotel are especially atmospheric, with intricate terracotta flooring and antique furnishings.

Villa Fiorita €€€€ *Via Pirandello 39, 98039 Taormina, tel: (0942) 24 122, email: villafioritahotel@libero.it.* Occupying a large villa near the Greek theatre, the Fiorita provides stylish accommodation and such amenities as a garden, solarium and swimming pool. The accommodation is all different, much of it with stunning views; if the hotel is not full when you arrive, you may want to look around for the room that best suits your tastes.

Villa Schuler €€ *Piazzetta Bastione 16, tel: (0942) 23 481, www. hotelvillaschuler.com.* The Schulers have been innkeepers at their ancestral villa since 1905, and continue to provide charming service, surroundings and the atmosphere of a private home. Most rooms have views down the coast, and the facilities include a lovely garden and a large, panoramic terrace. Minimum stay of two nights is required in high season. Free use of bikes for guests. Open Easter to October.

CATANIA

5 Balconi € *Via Plebiscito 133, tel: (0957) 234 534, www.5balconi.it.* On the second floor of a palazzo (with lift) and a stone's throw from the castle, this welcoming B&B has three individually furnished, homey guest rooms. The rooms share a bathroom and shower room, and have free WiFi. The owners (Rob, English, and Cristina, Sicilian) are hugely helpful hosts.

UNA Hotel Palace €€–€€€ *Via Etnea 218, tel: (095) 250 5111; www. unahotels.it.* Part of the UNA chain, this is a luxurious hotel on the main shopping street. Décor is minimalist with bold colours. Locals flock to the roof-garden bar for aperitifs and fine dining with views of Etna.

SIRACUSA

Gran Bretagna €€ *Via Savoia 21, Ortigia, tel: (0931) 68 765, www. hotelgranbretagna.it.* The surroundings are simple but the Gran Bretagna nonetheless attracts legions of return visitors who enjoy the good value and the Ortigia location. A few of the rooms have old frescoes and one has a terrace that looks over rooftops to the sea. The hotel is located a short distance from Piazza Duomo.

Grand Hotel €€€€ *Viale Mazzini 12, Ortigia, tel: (0931) 464 600, www.grandhotelortigia.it.* The Grand is the grandest hotel on Ortigia, and a recent refurbishment left period furnishings and a great deal of style intact, making this the choicest place to stay in Siracusa. The hotel overlooks Ortigia's yacht marina; the roof-garden restaurant has superb views. Private beach.

NOTO

Villa Mediterranea €€ *Viale Lido, Lido di Noto, tel: (0931) 812 330, www.villamediterranea.it.* While accommodation in old Noto is hard to come by, you'll find several places to stay in Lido di Noto, on the sea about 6km (4 miles) east. The Villa Mediterranea is one of the most pleasant hotels here, with simple but comfortable modern rooms and airy sea views. Across the road from the beach. 14 rooms.

RAGUSA

Locanda Don Serafino, €€–€€€ *Via XI Febbraio 15, Ragusa Ibla, tel: (0932) 222 0065, www.locandadonserafino.it.* This inviting boutique hotel, excavated from the rock face, with exposed stonework, has ten elegant guest rooms. The renowned restaurant, with a Michelin star, is 10 minutes' walk away.

Risveglio Ibleo € *Largo Camerina 3, Ragusa Ibla, tel: (0932) 247811, www.risveglioibleo.com.* This 19th-century palazzo has been converted into a B&B with four self-catering rooms in the main house and two rather less stylish ones at the back. The owner takes pride in serving you breakfast in his own dining room: Arab biscuits, thyme-flavoured *dolce*, fresh ricotta and fresh bread with home-made marmalade and Ragusa honey.

MÓDICA

Il Cavaliere € *Corso Umberto I 259, tel: (0932) 947219, www.palazzo ilcavaliere.it.* On the main street of Módica this is a lovely B&B with friendly owners in an elegant early-19th-century palazzo. Rooms are individually furnished and retain original features, such as frescoes and exposed stonework.

Palazzo Failla €€–€€€ *Via Blandini, 5, tel: (0932) 941059, www. palazzofailla.it.* Set in Módica Alta, this beguiling boutique hotel is suffused with Sicilian charm, left much as it was when the owners lived there – but made contemporary by the addition of a super star chef (see page 111). There are gorgeous rooms in the main building with frescoed ceilings, fine antiques and chandeliers, with more modern ones in the annexe.

AGRIGENTO

Villa Athena €€€€ *Passeggiata Archeologica 33, tel: (0922) 596 288, www.athenahotels.com.* Villa Athena enjoys a location that's sure to win the heart of anyone who can't get enough of ancient wonders – it's set in the Valley of the Temples, surrounded by gardens and olive trees. The 18th-century villa has been recently renovated and upgraded to 5 stars. Guest rooms are comfortably furnished, and some have terraces and astonishing views over the swimming pool and the surrounding ruins. This is one of Sicily's most popular hotels, so it's necessary to book well in advance.

SELINUNTE

Villa Mimosa € *La Rocchetta, Castelvetrano, Selinunte, tel: (0924) 44583, www.villamimosasicily.com.* This charming rustic villa is owned by Jackie Sirimanne, who is English but has lived in Sicily for years. Guest rooms with floral fabrics and original prints open on to a terrace and garden of jasmine and citrus trees. Jackie is hugely hospitable and more than happy to help plan your itinerary for the day.

MAZARA DEL VALLO

Mahara Hotel €€ *Lungomare San Vito, tel: (0923) 673800, www.maharahotel.it.* This excellent-value 4-star hotel on the seafront occupies an historic Marsala wine warehouse found by the Englishman John Hopps. Rooms have views of internal gardens and pool or the seafront. Facilities include a wellness centre, good fish restaurant and free shuttle bus to the beach.

SCIACCA

Grand Hotel Delle Terme €€€€ *Viale Nuove Terme 1, tel: (0925) 080462, www.grandhoteldelleterme.com.* This elegant seaside hotel carries on an ages-old Sciacca tradition, that of dispensing healing thermal treatments to clientele. Even if you don't require a full regimen, you can enjoy the relaxing thermal pool and use the spacious, well-equipped premises as a base from which to explore Agrigento, Sellinunte and other places along the southern coast.

TRÁPANI

Ai Lumi € *Corso Vittorio Emanuele 71; tel: (0923) 540 922; www.ailumi.it.* Located in the historic heart of town, this is an atmospheric family-run Bed and Breakfast within an 18th-century palazzo, where the rooms are built around a splendid courtyard full of character. Breakfasts are excellent, and the B&B has the distinct advantage of being in the same building (and under the same management) as the best restaurant in town, with 15 percent discount for guests.

ERICE

Elimo €€€ *Corso Vittorio Emanuele 75, tel: (0923) 869 377, www. hotelelimo.it.* This cosy 17th-century palazzo in the old town is a favourite weekend retreat for residents of Palermo. Rooms are warmly furnished with antiques and eclectic modern art, and many enjoy expansive views. If you have one of the viewless rooms facing the courtyard or surrounding streets, you can enjoy the sweeping vistas from the large terrace.

Moderno €€ *Corso Vittorio Emanuele 67, tel: (0923) 869 300, www. hotelmodernoerice.it.* An excellent restaurant, renowned for the local speciality fish couscous, is what draws many people to this tastefully furnished inn. Those who stay on though are pleased to discover an unusually attractive, well-run small hotel. The distinctive hand-woven rugs for which Erice is known carpet the halls and some of the guest rooms; other furnishings include antiques and country pieces.

EGADI ISLANDS (ISOLE EGADI)

Aegusa €€ *Via Garibaldi 11, Favignana, tel: (0923) 922 430, www. aegusahotel.it.* At the centre of the island this is a simple conversion of a palazzo, with spacious, comfortable rooms. Booking well ahead is essential during the summer months. Closed Nov–Mar.

Egadi €€ *Via Colombo 17, 91023 Favignana, tel: (0923) 921 232, www. albergoegadi.it.* Reservations are essential at this modest but stylish little hotel, which is popular with return visitors to the Egadi Islands. The restaurant is highly regarded; guests may be asked to opt for full board in August.

INDEX

Berlitz® pocket guide

Sicily

Fourth Edition 2013
Reprinted 2014

Written by Stephen Brewer
Updated by Susie Boulton
Edited by Sian Lezard
Art Editor: Tom Smyth
Series Editor: Tom Stainer
Production: Tynan Dean, Linton Donaldson
and Rebeka Davies

Photography credits: Dreamstime 2/3M;
Fotolia 103; iStockphoto 2TC, 4TL, 69; Neil
Buchan-Grant/Apa Publications 1, 2ML, 2TL,
2MC, 2/3T, 3TC, 2/3M, 2/3M, 4ML, 4ML,
4TL, 5MC, 4/5T, 5TC, 4/5M, 6(all), 7(all), 8, 10,
12, 12/13, 14, 16, 18, 20, 22, 24, 26, 28, 30, 31,
32, 34, 36, 37, 38, 39, 40, 42, 44, 45, 46, 48, 49,
50/51, 53, 54, 55, 56, 58, 59, 60, 61, 63, 64, 65,
66, 68, 70, 72, 73, 74, 75, 77, 78, 80/81, 82, 84,
86, 87, 88, 89, 90, 92, 93, 94, 96/97, 98, 100,
101, 105

Cover picture: 4 Corners Images

Every effort has been made to provide
accurate information in this publication,
but changes are inevitable. The publisher
cannot be responsible for any resulting
loss, inconvenience or injury.

Contact us

At Berlitz we strive to keep our guides as
accurate and up to date as possible, but if you
find anything that has changed, or if you have
any suggestions on ways to improve this guide,
then we would be delighted to hear from you.

Berlitz Publishing, PO Box 7910,
London SE1 1WE, England.
email: berlitz@apaguide.co.uk
www.insightguides.com/berlitz